JUST A SURVIVOR

Published in 1999 by
WOODFIELD PUBLISHING
Bognor Regis, West Sussex PO21 5EL, UK.

ISBN 0 873203 44 6

Just a Survivor

Phil Potts

Woodfield Publishing
~ WEST SUSSEX • ENGLAND ~

This Book Belongs to
A.F. Bayes-Chapman.

My Crew
Blondie • Ken • Johnnie • Phil *(The Author)* • Frank
Ossy

This story is dedicated to those who did not survive.

My Crew:

Johnny Austin (pilot)
Ken Webb (WoP/AG)
Blondie Hamilton (A/G)

Personal friends from Luton:

Gordon Caffell .... Army
John Coley .... Army
Aubrey (Brock) Denton .... Army
Rex Glenister .... Civilian
Stanley Grigg .... Army
Dennis Hawkes .... RAF
Keith Hibbert .... RAF
Fred Hobbs .... RAF
Rex Holmes .... Army
Jim Hubble .... RAF
Bill James .... RAF
Redfers Kenyon .... RAF
Harry Salter .... Army
Reg Shotbolt .... RAF
Norman Stronell .... RAF
Peter Thomas .... RAF
Philip Thomas .... RAF
Alan Underwood .... Royal Marines
Reg Verran .... RAF
Bob Verran .... RAF
John Wells .... Army
Bob Wilcockson .... RAF

List of Illustrations

Contents

The Author, 1943.

About the Author

PHILIP J. POTTS was born in Luton, Beds on 24th April, 1922. This is the story of his war from 1st September 1939 until he was released by the Royal Air Force in July 1946.

During the 1939/45 war there were many unsung heroes, who won no medals or awards for bravery, but in their own way served their country to the best of their ability, in many cases surviving great hardship, degradation and violation of civil liberties. The author was one of these.

Before the war he joined the civil defence, then known as Air Raid Precautions (ARP), and later the Fire Service at the local Aircraft factory where he worked. He joined the Royal Air Force for flying duties in 1941, obtained his Navigator's Wings in 1943 and flew with Bomber Command until shot down over France, soon after D-Day in 1944.

He spent the rest of the war in a prisoner of war camp just outside Berlin, having been force-marched from another camp at Bankau, Upper Silesia. Eventually he was repatriated to England at the end of May 1945, having spent six weeks in the hands of the advancing Russians.

| CHAPTER ONE |

The Run-up to War

My introduction to war started in the middle of 1938, when volunteers were requested from the local youth organisations to join "Air Raid Precautions" services, part of a national campaign to fill the ranks for all categories, Air Raid Wardens, Firemen, Ambulance and First Aiders and in my own case as a Messenger. At that time I was an active member of a Scout Group, and immediately volunteered, as I considered war was inevitable, and being too young for military service, decided that this was a way I could serve my country in the immediate future. I was at the time just 16 years of age.

This period before war actually started was a very active time for many of my own age group, most of us having already left school at fourteen, were now actively pursuing evening classes at the local College of Further Education, with a view to improving their qualifications, and a hope of more opportunities in later life. It should be remembered that at this time the United Kingdom was only just recovering from the 1930's slump and jobs of any kind were not easy to find. The prospectus for most courses entailed attendance on four or even five evenings per week, during the period September to April, each lasting two, three or in some instances up to four hours.

I was also working a full week as a management trainee at a well known engineering company in Luton, Hayward Tyler Co Ltd and in those days this called for a 5.5 day week of 47 hours, with one week holiday, plus statutory bank holidays of 6 days. Added to this were our usual pursuits in the fields of sports, Cricket, Football, Tennis, Roller Skating whilst continuing activities with the Scouts, of twice weekly meetings, week end camps in the summer, Church Parades, plus an active membership of the Church youth fellowship.

Now added to all this, training to become a fully qualified member of the Air Raid Precautions began, and thinking back some fifty years later, it is very difficult to imagine how we managed to fit all this into our daily lives.

This pattern continued until the end of 1938, and as the crisis deepened throughout the early part of 1939, and war became inevitable, it was evident that as I was a fully qualified member of Air Raid Precautions I would be required very soon after war was declared. In fact the call came very early on Friday 1st September 1939, and my first base was the local Police Station, which was the main command base, containing a communication office, with all services in attendance. As history will repeat, nothing much happened in these first few months of the war, but at least I received my initial training in the art of drinking beer at the pub opposite the station, ably aided and abetted by members of the local constabulary.

Also on 1st September colleagues of mine at the company where I worked, were also "Called Up" into the Territorial Army, and most of these were subsequently captured with the

Bedfordshire and Hertfordshire Regiment at the fall of Singapore, and became prisoners of the Japanese. I relate this because there but for the grace of God go I! Earlier in 1939 I had with these same colleagues also volunteered for the Territorial Army but being under age, my parents refused to sign the consent form. Only one returned from captivity.

| CHAPTER 2 |

From Dunkirk to the Blitz

The Phoney War and Dunkirk

After the initial impact of war being declared, a sort of normality returned, everybody continued with their everyday work and nothing much changed. Places of entertainment which had originally closed, now began to re-open. The 'blackout' was severely maintained and restrictions on headlights and other lighting was imposed. Other noticeable changes became more evident particularly in dress, with more and more people appearing in Navy, Army or Royal Air Force uniforms, with the civil defence and other services easily identified. This state of affairs continued until May 1940, when the collapse of France and the British Expeditionary Force's retreat from Dunkirk dramatically changed everything and this country was very much at war and alone. Everyone you met had no other topic of conversation, and very soon the possibility of invasion of this country by the German forces became very real and it became evident that this country was now in a real war, and activity became much more serious, with preparations to repel invasion taking priority.

As this is intended as a personal account of my own involvement in the war, at this same time there were two changes in my own life. Firstly I changed my employment and joined the local aircraft company Percival Aircraft, and so began my association with flying and the aircraft industry which has lasted to this day. Secondly I was also transferred in my duties within the ARP services and was attached to the Fire Service, still as a messenger, and located at one of the satellite stations, which for practical reasons had been scattered throughout the town, to give greater cover in the face of anticipated air raids. My duties includeded travelling out with a crew, when an alert was sounded, to one of the many 'dispersal sites' in and around the town. With the equipment no longer all in one place, the possibility of it all being damaged or destroyed by a single bomb was avoided.

The Battle Of Britain

Although by mid summer the south of England was regularly being attacked by the German Luftwaffe, Luton remained comparatively safe and quiet, but as the bombing raids extended into London, it became inundated by refugees from that city. Rows of empty houses, unoccupied for some considerable time, were now rented, and where previously there had been a surplus of accommodation, soon it became very difficult to obtain anything at all. It was not until the end of August 1940 that Luton suffered its first blow, when a string of bombs dropped by a bomber being chased out of London, straddled the town, doing considerable damage at Vauxhall Motors, the Park Street area and continuing in the direction of Farley Hill, with a quite considerable death toll. Although scheduled to report to Vauxhall Motors in the event of an incident, due to security at the Airport I was not allowed to leave, and thus my first involvement in an action had to be deferred until a later date. Some years after this raid I met my wife, and found that she and her family had to be evacuated from Farley Hill, due to an unexploded bomb, and spent the night at a local hotel.

This book is not intended to cover the Battle of Britain, which has been well documented by others more qualified to do so than I – but my memories of those days; the vapour trails, the stray fighters landing on the airfield, remain as a vivid in my memory as Winston Churchill's statement: "Never in the field of human conflict was so much owed by so many to so few". Although this was a most exciting period of my life, I will not try to emulate others by attempting to rewrite this part of our history.

The Blitz

As August receded and the famous victory was won (now commemorated in annual remembrance services) on the 15th September, the Battle of Britain was over and the blitz on London and other major cities - Liverpool, Manchester, Coventry, Bristol, Exeter began. There were air raid warnings on most nights, and my own activities with the Fire Service increased, but although much scurrying backwards and forwards took place, on the occasions when bombs did drop in the area, I was never on duty. For the rest of my life I will remember the familiar drone of German bombers as they travelled over Luton on their deadly missions, and the night when Coventry suffered so badly, remains as a horrible dream. No deliberate raids were ever made on Luton, which was surprising, when you consider that Vauxhall Motors (who subsequently manufactured the Churchill tank), Percival

Aircraft (later to make Mosquito aircraft), Skefko (international suppliers of ball bearings), Laporte (a large chemical company) and Commer Cars (whose trucks and light vehicles were known everywhere) were obvious targets. Nevertheless, a considerable amount of damage was caused, perhaps more by accident than design, particularly in the Vauxhall Motors and Airport areas, by stray Bombers releasing their loads indiscriminately.

During this period, I witnessed an event which gave rise to a strange coincidence at a much later date, after I had joined the Royal Air Force. From my bedroom window I was watching an aircraft coming in to land with its landing light on (at the time there was a Defiant Night Fighter Squadron based at Luton Airport) when a huge explosion was heard and a flash lit up the sky. Subsequently it was revealed that this was a land mine dropped by a German Aircraft, which fortunately fell on the airfield and did virtually no damage to the buildings. In 1943, while undergoing Pilot training in Canada, I was talking to a New Zealand Commissioned Air Gunner, now also undergoing Pilot training, and it transpired that he had not only served with the Defiant Squadron at Luton, but had been gunner in the very aircraft I had been watching. It is a small world indeed!

Another land mine, dropped presumably by the same aircraft, landed virtually in the middle of the Percival Aircraft Factory, but was not discovered until the following morning, when all transport was stopped and no access allowed to the airport. Fortunately, a specialist Naval Lieutenant, who was subsequently decorated for his devotion to duty during the blitz, made the mine safe. Later, Jack Cunningham, the Local Defence Force (Home Guard) C/O and a long time acquaintance of my family, was awarded the George Medal along with the local Inspector of Police, for bravery and devotion to duty. At the beginning of the war Jack had been the Security Officer at Percival's and when the Local Defence Force was formed in May after the fall of France, he became the Commanding Officer with the rank of Major, mainly due to his First World War record and service, in which he was awarded the Distinguished Service Order. Some five years later we had much more in common when I returned after my period in a prisoner of war camp, an experience he had endured during the latter part of the 1914-1918 war.

On a lighter note, during this period I started my first steps in ballroom dancing, attending Miss Brown's dancing academy and local dance halls at every opportunity when I was not on duty. In those early days of the war, even though there were air raids most nights, the local arenas, The George Hotel, and Winter Assembly Hall particularly flourished. I was also a regular attendee at Christ Church Youth Fellowship, where activity was again at a high level, in both the Church and the hall opposite in Inkerman Street, which to this day holds happy memories.

The major factor in the day-to-day life of the inhabitants of Luton at that time was the length of the working day. Many extra hours, often seven days per week, were worked, as production of all kinds increased. In my own particular case, this meant aircraft, as the requirements of the Royal Air Force increased. At the time Percival Aircraft were making Airspeed Oxfords, a twin-engined training and communication aircraft.

During that period until the end of 1940, when work and ARP duties allowed, normal activities resumed, and even until the autumn of 1941, my attendance at the local Technical College continued, although on a restricted scale. Even at times a visit to the local cinema, which had been reopened, was fitted into my busy schedule, and these and the pubs and dance halls were doing a flourishing trade. Because of daylight saving, the clocks were at double summer time even in the winter, everybody started work that much earlier, and subsequently most evening activities also ended much earlier, to enable people to go home, hopefully before the first air-raid warning sounded, and often there were more than one per night. I am sure that nobody living at the time will ever forget the doleful sound of the warnings and intense relief when the all clear was heard.

This was the pattern that prevailed until the end of 1940 and into the early months of 1941, and as each day passed more and more it became obvious from the nightly news bulletins, that this was going to be a long hard war, and very rarely were any glad tidings received. Coinciding with the fall of France, had been the debacle resulting in the loss of Norway, and with Russia entering the war on the side of Germany, things did look bleak. The actions in the Middle East were far from encouraging, and with the shipping losses, particularly in the Atlantic increasing, there was at that time very little to cheer us, except our own good humour. It was at this moment in British history that the courage and fortitude of the people, especially those who lived in blitzed cities and towns, shone through, and never in my lifetime have I known such comradeship, with everybody prepared to help one another.

It would be appropriate at this stage to introduce my good friend Brian Owen, who, at Christmas 1940, announced that he had volunteered and been accepted by the Royal Air Force to train as a Wireless Operator/Air Gunner, and would be enlisting very shortly, having already been 'sworn in' (the term used when one swears allegiance to King and Country). We had known each other since school days, starting in 1933 at

Waller Street School, and continued to work together at Hayward Tyler, where he was an apprentice. He subsequently completed two tours of operations in Bomber Command during the peak of the offensive in Autumn/Winter of 1943 and the first months of 1944, which period included the Battle of Berlin, and for his services was awarded the Distinguished Flying Medal by His Majesty The King. Forty years later we are still in contact and see each other, but not now on such a regular basis.

By the end of May 1941, the Blitz on London was coming to an end and culminated in a raid early in the month, which coincided with a war time Cup Final at Wembley between Arsenal and Liverpool, which I attended with my brother Tom. Because of difficulties of getting away from the stadium, we eventually had to travel into London (Victoria) before we could obtain a coach home and it was with a sigh of relief when we heard the news the next morning, that we were not stranded in the city overnight. It was one of the heaviest raids of the Blitz!

As the raids became less frequent my need to remain in the ARP was not so essential, and therefore I joined the works Fire Brigade as a part-time Fireman. This entailed instruction and training on several lunch times every week, being on all night duty on some days of the week, occasional week ends, but more importantly being on call at all times while at the Airport.

This was a stimulating period, but with the momentous events taking place in other areas of the war, particularly in North Africa, and the fact that because Germany had attacked Russia in the spring of 1941 the threat of invasion of our country had receded, my thoughts often strayed to the armed forces, and especially the Royal Air Force. By this time many of my friends, particularly from Scouting days, had already enlisted into the services (mostly the Navy) and in fact some had already been killed in action. In early 1941, another colleague, Jim Hubble, and I applied to enlist in the Royal Air Force for flying duties. We were rejected on the grounds that, working in the aircraft industry, we were considered to be in 'reserved occupations'. So life had to be accepted as it was, work, the Fire Service, and whatever other activity could be squeezed into an already crowded schedule.

But this could not last, even though I had resumed my first love by playing Football for the works team plus the odd game of cricket, in October 1941 Jim and I volunteered again, and this time were accepted for flying duties in the Royal Air Force Volunteer Reserve (RAFVR). Our final assessment was at Oxford for two days of tests, medicals, and all other requirements to assess our suitability. Having been accepted we were 'sworn in', and sent home on deferred service to await our call up, which we were advised would be in approximately 3 - 4 months. Jim was killed in October 1944, although I was not aware of this until very much after the event and only after I returned from Germany in June 1945. During this period of waiting we proudly wore our badge and RAFVR tie and joined the Air Training Corp (ATC), a recently formed body, to learn the rudiments of Air Force training including Morse Code, which was of great help when we actually enlisted. Another essential was to have teeth repaired to the standard required of the Royal Air Force, but most fortunately at their expense. It was at this time that I first met John Austin, already a member of the ATC, who subsequently became my pilot when we operated together in a Lancaster Bomber. Sadly, he was to die when our aircraft was shot down in August 1944. More about that later.

The momentous events of Pearl Harbour brought the USA into the war in December 1941, but this made little change to my own circumstances, the pattern remained as in the previous few months, with the exception that I waited eagerly for the day when I would enlist.

Very early in 1942 came the news of the fall of Singapore, and we learnt that some of our local regiments had been stationed there, and therefore those colleagues of mine who had enlisted in the Territorial Army would be involved. Subsequently we heard that they had become prisoners of war of the Japanese – but it was very much later that we learned of their brutal and inhuman treatment. Only one ever came home, Bill Emmett, and he had the most amazing escape, having been rescued from a submarine, which was sunk while transporting prisoners of war to mainland Japan.

| CHAPTER 3 |

Joining the Royal Air Force

The great day for me (but not, might I add, for my parents) arrived at last and on Easter Monday, 6th April 1942, I arrived at the Air Crew Recruitment Centre at Lords Cricket Ground, St Johns Wood to begin my new career. I should add that the previous two weeks had been a very busy period, tidying up the loose ends of my civilian life, plus the many farewell parties, and I particularly remember one given by my friends and colleagues in the Fire Service. By this time having worked for Percival Aircraft for 18 months I had established myself in the Purchasing Department in a Junior Buyers position, being involved in the buying of products used in the commercial side of business. This was a career that I pursued when returned to the company after leaving the Royal Air Force.

Little did I know what to expect, but in those first few days I learned pretty fast, and again my scouting and camping activities, which if nothing else had taught me how to mix, stood me in good stead.

There is nothing like services for organising your life, "Do This" "Do That" "Don't Do That" "Go There" "Get In Line" "Get Out of Line" "Fall In" "Fall Out". We received our kit, and believe it or not, a tailor was in attendance to ensure our uniforms fitted! We were inoculated, we were vaccinated, we were given blood tests, we were medically examined, we learnt what an FFI was, our eyes were retested and those who required remedial treatment were segregated. It was surprising how many required this treatment for lazy reflexes. Night visions tests were included in this early bombardment and mine being classified as "Above Average". I was soon earmarked then and at a later date, to locate obstacles in the blackout, particularly the back doors of pubs. To ensure our boots fitted (shoes for Air Crew came much later), we were instigated into the mysteries of drill, and under what appeared to be the sadistic eye of the physical training Corporals, we were exercised until muscles which we did not know we had, ached. Our accommodation was in the luxury flats in and around St. Johns Wood Road, which had all been commandeered by the Royal Air Force for the duration, and our Mess Hall was in the restaurant of Regents Park Zoo. Animals were still in residence, but we were segregated from them for eating purposes.

For the first few days we were not allowed out of our billets in the evenings, but at the end of the first week we were advised that Saturday afternoon was free and the six of us who had joined up from Luton, were able to go home for a few hours, returning on the last train, and entering our billet by the back door. On the one occasion that we were forced to enter by the front, the Corporal on duty was Joe Payne a well known Luton footballer, who overlooked our lateness. In the service for only a short time and already breaking the rules!

Our indoctrination into the service continued with lectures, drill, PT and those of us who had already learned the rudiments of Morse Code signalling were able to avoid this part of the training after passing the required standard. From the day we joined, we were impressed that if we gained our coveted "wings", then we would be appointed either Commissioned or Non Commissioned Officers, and an enormous amount of our basic training had this in view. This initial training lasted for four weeks and at the end of this period, we had been trained to the extent that "drill" was no longer a foreign language and the apoplexy of our instructors had been reduced to more normal proportions. As there was some congestion, due to causes unknown, we were not sent to Initial Training Wing at the completion of this basic training, but instead were sent to another reception centre at Brighton for an extension of our training. Again the accommodation was of the very best and the most prestigious hotels in the town had been commandeered for the Royal Air Force, and we were billeted in the mighty Grand Hotel with our Head Quarters building the Hotel Metropol next door. Parades were held in the forecourt of the hotel, which contained seven main floors, but above these were the old servants quarters, and this is where my room was the eighth floor, and no lifts in operation. One soon became adept at running up and down stairs, as being late on parade was a most heinous crime, punishable by extra duties. Fortunately there were more extra duties handed out than there were men to do them. This was my first visit to Brighton, and despite the restrictions of the service, and the fact that there was barbed wire defending the beaches against invasion this was a most pleasant introduction to service life, and a memory which has remained with me. It was here that I had my first close encounter with a German FW190, which used to hop over the channel with two 500 lb bombs attached to their wings, and drop them indiscriminately on coastal towns. It was good to know that our own fighter wings were doing the same over the other side, with even deeper penetration. On the occasion in question two aircraft were flying parallel to the shore, each hopping over the two piers, but fortunately they did not attack Brighton.

We completed our training. By this time we were quite experienced in drill procedures, and we were advised that we would be posted: this was a term we would soon come to know very well. We were going to No. 8 ITW (Initial Training Wing) at Newquay in Cornwall and were to leave in a few days. Two days before departure, a very kind PTI took us on a scorching hot day, for a run along the promenade, to a gap made in the barbed wire defences, and invited us to swim in the sea – an invitation we could not refuse. Incidentally, I had only just learned to swim at Brighton, because one was faced with the situation that until one could, one was not permitted to play any other sport. With no protection from the sun and no towel to dry ourselves, when we left Brighton, carrying full packs to march to the railway station, there were very many sore backs and shoulders. Remember that sunburn is a crime in the forces, so none of us dared complain.

No. 8 Initial Training Wing, Newquay 1942

After an overnight journey, where the train seemed to divert into every siding and station in Hampshire, Dorset, Devon and Cornwall, we eventually reached our destination in the early morning. One memory is passing through Plymouth and seeing the extensive damage due to the German raids. If we needed further proof or incentive to gain our Wings and avenge this destruction, then this was it.

This was where our basic training began, prior to actually flying – our ultimate goal. Again, the Royal Air Force had commandeered all the major hotels, with No. 7 ITW at one end of the town, and No. 8 at the other. My home for the next twelve weeks was to be the Edgecliffe Hotel, overlooking Fistral beach, and within only a few minutes walk of the town centre and shops. This was a situation I had never known previously, holidays until the war had consisted of one weeks camp with the scouts each year, and although most enjoyable and in most cases constructive, did not compare with the anticipation I knew now - June, July, August and part of September in Newquay. Little did I know then how much my Scout training would mean to me later.

Our first lesson was to absorb the objects of ITW, which were, firstly to be trained in the basics for our ultimate courses, Navigation, Theory of Flight, Aircraft Recognition, Signals, Meteorology, Armaments and all other relevant subjects. Secondly, to learn discipline and Air Force Law, which included hours of drilling, with and without rifles, and parades of all types. Thirdly, fitness was an essential part of our training and this included PT on the beach every day, despite the weather immediately followed by a swim in the sea. Added to this were sports of all kinds mostly played on the beach, plus cross country running and tennis. We worked six days a week, and after church parade on Sunday morning, we were free for the rest of the day, did not have a room inspection and thus no bed making, but there was much to do, studying to ensure success in this part of our training, which would mean promotion and extra pay. As mentioned above sport was an essential part of our every day, and as our Commanding Officer was Sq/Ldr A.H. Fabian, an amateur international footballer and a first class county

No.8 ITW, Newquay 1942 (Author third row from front, 6th from left)

cricketer this was inevitable. His favourite ploy was to approach one of the Flights late in the afternoon, instructing them to have a team on the beach 30 minutes after the evening meal to play his team at Softball. Nobody ever refused.

Besides the lectures, which were an integral part of our course, various others on a multitude of subjects were a regular part of our daily curriculum. One in particular remains in my memory, given by Joe Binks a previous holder of the world one mile running record, and at the time a sporting correspondent for the News of the World. During the course of his talk he stated that it was most unlikely that anyone would be able to run a mile in under four minutes. He would have been surprised if he were alive today, to see the present times regularly performed over this distance.

Because of the very full life we were living, both academic and sporting, plus the regular drill instruction, as can be imagined our nightlife was reduced to a minimum, and by lights out, which was at ten o'clock, we were ready for bed. One enthusiastic member of my flight tried unsuccessfully to induce me to join him each morning on an early swim, but my bed always won, until the morning when he came to wake me after he had been rather than before. A very rude wakening indeed! This was Double Summer Time, a wartime measure, at a time of the year when it did not get dark until 11 o'clock. How we looked forward to Saturdays, we could stay out until midnight, with dances to go to, though regrettably there was a shortage of ladies, due to the large numbers of Army and Air Force personnel in town. As readers may have noticed, I have not mentioned family or girlfriends, and the truth is that, at this particular time, I was not a very good correspondent, and apart from a regular letter to my mother, few others ever heard from me and it was not my intention to have any steady relationships during wartime.

Although we did not compete very much outside our own flights, on one occasion I had the honour to represent the Wing against the Army at an inter-service sports day. I ran in a 4 x 440 yard relay race, which we won, and I became the proud owner of a trophy in the form of miniature Cornish Stone Lighthouse – one of the few awards I received during my Air Force career.

Some four weeks before the end of the course, and about two weeks before he was killed in an aircraft crash, we were inspected by the Duke of Kent, then an Air Commodore in Training Command. I was one of the cadets he spoke to on this parade, and was very much aware of his perfume, something I had read about but never experienced.

As we approached the end of our course, the main topic of conversation was "Would we pass". Yes, we passed and proudly sewed on the emblems of an LAC (Leading Aircraftsman), and looked forward to an increase in pay. A few days after this event, we proceeded on seven days leave, the first after nearly six months in the Service, and you can imagine that the tan I had gained after the previous six months in the sun, was greatly admired by those at home.

Grading School: RAF Sywell, Northampton

All good things come to an end, and on returning to Newquay after my leave some two weeks later I was posted to Grading School at Sywell, where we were to receive our first flying instruction. This system had been introduced to assess aptitude and to divide cadets into categories of Pilot, Navigator or Bomb Aimer. It was known as the 'PNB scheme', and allowed for approximately 12 hours of flying each. We arrived in Sywell in early October, for many, this was to be their first experience of flying. I was one of the few who had already taken to the air, having been fortunate enough to be permitted to fly in an Airspeed Oxford, off the production line at Percival Aircraft in Luton, with Chief test pilot Flt/Lt Leonard Carruthers, RAF at the controls. This was arranged soon after I had been selected for the Royal Air Force and a few weeks before I enlisted.

This was an exciting time. Each of us was allocated to a flying instructor for our daily instruction in the basic trainer then in use, the one and only Tiger Moth, manufactured by the De Havilland Company at Hatfield. Although first produced long before the war, it was probably the most widely used training aircraft ever. To say that I was not a natural pilot would be an understatement – but at least I did as well as the rest of the flight! When we were not flying, our ground training continued, particularly in those areas applicable to flying, and it was here that the earlier lectures on "theory of flight" began to register, and what earlier had been just statistics now became reality.

This course lasted for three weeks and 12 hours flying time, and it has always been my regret that no Log Book was issued for those hours. At the end of this time we were sent on two weeks leave, but were not told how we fared, or the results of our selection. One positive fact was that, having been granted flying pay, additional to our daily rate during this period, we were advised that it would be consolidated into our pay and would continue until we were advised otherwise.

Transit Camp: Heaton Park, Manchester

Our two weeks leave was extended to three, and we then reported to our new home, which was a huge transit camp on the outskirts of Manchester, for trainee aircrew awaiting transportation overseas to the Commonwealth Air Training Schools in Canada, USA and South Africa. This was supposed to be a short stay camp, but for those of us arriving in November 1942, there was an unusual delay. Little did we know at the time that our arrival in Manchester coincided with the Allied landings in North Africa, taking all available transport with it. It was some time afterwards that I found out that my brother Joe and brother-in-law Alf were involved in these landings. It was also a time for reunion with John Austin who had enlisted with me in April, who was billeted in private accommodation nearby. On a social visit one evening it was quite a surprise when the landlord advised that he was associated with a Jack Potts in his insurance business. After an exchange of details it was established that he was one of my cousins on my father's side of the family.

This was also my first experience of living in a Nissan Hut, which after the comfort we had experienced so far in our billets, came as rather a nasty culture shock, and a reminder that life in the Royal Air Force could be rather uncomfortable. Those who have not experienced this way of living, until such time as you accept that there is only one point i.e. the middle of the hut where you will find any heat, this being the place where the coke burning stove is positioned, then you will suffer unnecessarily. In my hut there was a South African spending his first winter in England who spent all his time, including most of the night, feeding the stove and his bed was positioned so that his feet were virtually in the fire. As most people will appreciate Manchester is not the driest place in the UK, and keeping ones clothes and kit dry and in good order was an additional hazard.

Instead of a transit camp, Heaton Park became a semi permanent base for several more weeks, with the authorities thinking up various ways and means of keeping us amused, which for some included a short stay in Bridgenorth on survival exercises. After our experience with the Nissan Huts in Heaton Park this was not too difficult.

Being so close to Manchester, we had no problems in amusing ourselves in our spare time and again the Hotels, Pubs, Dance Halls and numerous service clubs were very welcoming, and the cinemas having the latest film releases plus Richard Tauber the famous singer appearing at one of the local theatres, we were well catered for. For a period of time I had as a close companion, Jim Hubble with whom I first enlisted, but he had been slightly ahead of me having been called up two weeks earlier and also avoided delays in leaving ACRC (Air Crew Recruiting Centre) to go to his Initial Training Wing. Sadly he was killed in a flying accident in October 1944, although I was not to know this until after I returned to England from my sojourn in Germany. To this day I still have a soft spot for Manchester, although my visits have been limited. During this period we were advised of our selection of Air Crew Category, and to my great surprise I had been selected for Pilot Training, which most importantly meant that I retained my flying pay. All other categories had this removed until such time as they resumed flying.

In Transit

At last at the end of 1942 movements began again, and at the beginning of January 1943, I with my close colleagues found ourselves on a draft to Blackpool, where we were to be "kitted out" for travel to our ultimate destination, South Africa. This stay in Blackpool, with its many attractions, even in wartime, remains a happy memory, and whenever I visit today, usually at the Royal Air Forces Association Annual Conference, these memories come flooding back. However, the interlude ended not on a boat to South Africa but in the local RAF Hospital at Weedon for a minor operation, which meant that I lost contact with my close friends, and in fact never did see South Africa or them again.

I must admit that I had not been looking forward to a six week ocean trip, and so it came as a great relief, when after release from hospital, I was very quickly on a draft to Canada, via dear old Heaton Park, Manchester. My documents, although I did not know it then, had unfortunately already gone to South Africa, and took rather a long time to catch up. We left Manchester very late one evening and in the morning mist had our first sight of the Firth of Clyde and a glimpse of our new home for the following 8 to 10 days MV Empress of Scotland a P&O cruise liner of some 26,000 tons that in peacetime had been on the Far East run and had changed its name at the outbreak of war from Empress of Japan.

It would not be true to say that the voyage was uneventful. We were at sea for seven days, using the southerly route to New York to avoid the worst of the weather. If this was not the worst, I am grateful that I never experienced the worst. Of those on board, which included our own contingent of RAF trainees, there were also some 1,000 young sailors going to America to collect Liberty Boats, which the American Government had made available to us, and for the first three days at least 75% of all personnel on board were seasick – very seasick – and this included one sailor who had served for 30 years!

Included in the naval contingent was the younger brother of my brother-in-law, who, being one of those who was very ill, suggested that it might be a good idea if we swapped uniforms, as I had not been affected! The sea was rough, unbelievably rough, and the vessel pitched and tossed in every conceivable direction. For those who were not ill, petrified perhaps but not seasick, those first three days were heaven. No queues for the mess deck, as much food as you could eat, and the freedom of the boat. The journey to the mess deck was a real test of character and stomach, as from our own quarters we had to proceed through the crew's quarters (mostly Chinese) and then through the laundry, with all the steam, smells and odours which emanate from that, and along a long corridor full of the smell of cooking and food being prepared. It took a strong stomach to withstand that assault course, and many did not make it to the end. The only item I found to be unpalatable was the beer in the canteen. It must have been very bad for me to refuse it. On one occasion I was sitting on the upper deck eating a bar of chocolate, when a figure rose behind me, absolutely green in the face, and begged me to go somewhere else to eat, adding that he would sooner die peacefully. As people recovered, the queues on the mess deck lengthened – we knew our exclusive 'club' could not last, but it was pleasant while it did.

Eventually some time early one morning, we awoke to see signs of land, which we were advised was New York, and soon the Statue of Liberty and then the famous harbour came into view with the skyscrapers of the city in the background. A wonderful sight, and one that today's airline travellers never see. We were ferried across the river after mooring, and had our first view of a New York Railway station (I think Grand Central, but am not certain) and eventually boarded a train, which was scheduled to take us to our first stop in Canada, at Moncton, New Brunswick, which was a transit camp for Air Crew to be trained and for those returning after completing theirs. Our journey was anything but uneventful. When we arrived at Boston, Maine, still in the USA, our train broke down and the security officers had to place a guard round the station to keep the local population from taking us to their homes. They were of the opinion that, being in the Royal Air Force, we must have all fought in the "Battle of Britain" and were consequently war heroes... How wrong they were.

| CHAPTER 4 |

Canada, 1943

Upon arrival in Moncton, after the usual preliminaries we were advised that our stay would be brief, before we were posted to our various Flying Schools, which were spread across Canada, with some in the USA. In the event we stayed for only two weeks, but it gave us our first taste of Canadian hospitality, which after the wartime restrictions in Britain came as a wonderful surprise. On my first night out, due to the richness of the food, I was actually sick! As New Brunswick was a dry state (no alchohol on sale) it could only be the food. For the whole of my stay in Canada such hospitality was invariably encountered, and is a fond memory of a wonderful country, inhabited by the most generous and warm people.

As a young boy growing up I had always been interested in the history of Canada, particularly the west, and it came as a pleasant surprise that I was to do my Elementary Flying at Bowden, Alberta, which is situated almost exactly half way between Calgary in the south of the province and Edmonton in the north. To reach Bowden we travelled by train (a four day journey) and the wonders of Canada evolved around us as we went. Our train had been specially prepared as a troop transporter, and apart from driver and guard there were no other

No. 2 A.O.S. Edmonton 1943 (Author third from right front row)

staff. As you will appreciate, catering, sleeping and everything else involved in our journey was very much a do-it-yourself job. The snow was still heavily on the ground, and apart from stops in various towns, everything seemed an unending carpet of white. This scenery was certainly breathtaking at times, and as we travelled round some parts of the Great Lakes we wondered at the efforts and engineering feats of those who laid the first railways. However, sitting in a train for four days, and particularly the whole day it took to pass through the prairies was not the most exhilarating of experiences, but it certainly gave a good picture of the vastness of the country.

Elementary Flying School, Bowden

To say that this was the highlight of my career would be a major misstatement. When we first arrived, the snow was still thick on the ground, and the faithful Tiger Moths were fitted with skis instead of wheels. Add to this the glare of very bright sunlight, which was really very beautiful, but to an untrained pilot hardly made flying any easier, particularly when trying to land. Even when the snow receded, and we were again using landing wheels and not skis, although I had mastered many of the techniques of flying, it became very obvious, even to me, that I would never make a pilot. As my instructor said with great feeling "You have the feet of a Bloody Elephant!" and even I could not contradict that, as by this time I was flying in slippers instead of boots. I always knew when I really had upset him as he would take over the controls, go into a series of violent aerobatics and after some five to ten minutes pass control back to me saying "That feels better!"

To cut a sad and sorry story short, after about six weeks training the Chief Instructor, having tested me, decided that I would not make a Pilot, and it would be to everybody's advantage – particularly the Royal Air Force's – if I remustered.

During this period of intense training, we did have some free time, and it was at a dance at the local town of Innisfail, that I met Margaret and her friend Jean. Although my efforts at actual flying had been most disappointing and frustrating, my ground work had been very well above standard, which proved advantageous at a later date, and all in all the few weeks spent at Bowden were a very happy time, and remembered in after years as a good memory.

I was finally in RAF terms "washed out" (ceased training) just two days before my 21st birthday, and as I was granted a few days leave. I was able to travel to Edmonton where Margaret lived, and we spent my birthday together, although I did not tell her this until the day after. As she was a lady, she did not use the appropriate language and tell me what she thought! We made up for this omission when we celebrated her own 21st some three months later.

What followed is one of the most wonderful periods of my life. The Air Force decided that my new career should be as a Navigator, and while waiting to be sent to an appropriate training school, I was posted to the Manning Depot (recruiting centre) in Edmonton. All the CT's (ceased training) were in one flight, and for a period of one month we enjoyed all the benefits of a situation where nobody knew what to do with us. As long as we did not misbehave, we were free to enjoy the wonderful Canadian hospitality and so for us the world took on a very rosy hue – at least for a while.

It was here that I first made contact with the members of the Royal Australian Air Force, who were either in transit, having gained their "wings" or like us were waiting for a new posting, having remustered. As Cadets under training, we were treated exactly as new entries, which entailed being back in camp by 10 pm but with the help of our new Australian friends we overcame this problem by borrowing the overcoats of those with 'wings' and casually walking past the guards in one of their groups. Every morning we met in the "Bull ring" a building in the centre, and after roll call, nobody was ever missing, our Sergeant (a real human being) briefed us on the day's programme. This was rarely accomplished, as always one of us would complain that we had missed breakfast, and our human Sergeant would march us out of camp to rectify this omission. We did on one occasion receive a nasty shock, when quite unusually an efficient drill Sergeant took over, and we found out later that he had served 12 years in the Brigade of Guards in England.

Whilst out one afternoon having a drink in one of the Hotels (drink was severely restricted), with three of my friends an incident occurred straight out of a "B" movie. We were approached by two rough-looking men who asked us if we would go to the Liquor Store and buy a licence, which they would pay for, and then buy as much liquor as this would allow. Hard liquor could only be obtained in this way, and as they had bought us each a beer, we though it was the least we could do. However, having met our part of the bargain, we attempted to move on, but they insisted we return to their rooms for a drink. Their rooms were in a seedy part of town, in a tenement block with an old lady at the bottom of the stairs, checking who was going in and out. The first words to hit our ears, when we arrived upstairs were, "Where's the dame? ...She's gone!" We left as soon as it was polite to do so, but by then we had established that these men were all trappers who spent months in the Northern territories, and when they returned to town were only interested in two things: wine and women. An interesting experience nevertheless!

Edmonton in 1943 was a beautiful city, with many open spaces, good restaurants, dance halls, swimming pools, pool rooms and bowling alleys, all of which in my first month were used to the full. By this time I had got to know Margaret better, and often used to spend weekends with her at her parents farm on the edge of the city, where they farmed and bred racehorses. I imagined that this idyllic situation could not last, but when posting came through I was sent to the Navigation School at the aerodrome in Edmonton, and so began probably the most satisfying period of my Air Force career. The only sad part was that a great Australian friend, Steve had been sent on a Bomb Aimers course at a different location. We had not known each other very long but had found that we had a lot in common.

No. 2 Air Observer School, Edmonton, Alberta

We worked hard! The course was of twenty weeks duration, which had been condensed from a pre-war period of eighteen months, and used the Avro Anson for our training exercises. Unlike my Pilot training, Navigation to me came very easily, and although it is not nice to boast, without effort I was able to compete with the best, without effort. However this did not always follow in my class work, even in my studies before the war I had always been lax on homework and again because I did no more work than necessary, I finished up bottom in ground work, and nearly top of the flight in flying. Despite this I qualified and duly received my half wing as a Navigator, at the completion of the course.

My memories of this twenty weeks in my life are indelibly printed on me, and is a period I shall never easily forget. Flying by day and night mostly in clear skies, with the background of the Rocky Mountains on view to the West, the beautiful wooded areas with numerous lakes to the North and the prairies and farms to the East and South. It was almost impossible to get lost, as the main railway lines, the Canadian Pacific and the Canadian National were clearly visible at all times, and if all else failed you could fly low over any town and read the name on the grain elevator. Aids which made navigation easy, something we would find with a nasty shock when we started flying over the British Isles and subsequently over Germany. Classwork and physical fitness were very much a part of our daily life, and as stated earlier as I have always had a capacity for absorbing information given at lectures, I did not work as hard studying as I might have done, and thus only just got home on ground work, which even entailed retaking one examination.

Navigation with all the navigational aids available was never a problem, and the only one was the Anson Aircraft, which being full of projectiles, was a constant source of danger to my head and on one occasion my front teeth when holding a camera, during photographic exercises. Physical exercises under our Canadian instructor became an absolute bore, until we convinced him that we could achieve just as much, or even better results, by playing football, to which after he watched us in action, he agreed and it was football only from then on! As we reached the end of our course while flying at night, we had the most marvellous views of the Aurora Borealis (the northern lights) which were most impressive.

The last trip during daylight was a flight North towards the Lesser Slave Lake, which is quite uninhabited country, covered with lakes and forests, and here again I proved just how unsuited I was as a Pilot. The staff Pilot who I had got to know quite well, during the course, handed over the controls to me while he went back to check the radio, and as I meandered all over the sky, I realised he had returned and was standing behind me, with the widest grin on his face. We agreed that I was not exactly a born Pilot!

This was a most happy period, the comradeship in our flight of 30 airmen both UK and Canadian was excellent, and my own flying partner, an Australian Fred Thee, became a real friend as well as comrade. Fred did however surpass himself on one occasion when in his log he estimated 7/10ths cloud when in fact it was virtually a clear sky. He had mistaken the Canadian Rocky Mountains to our West as cloud. It took a long while for him to live this down. An interesting side to this friendship came during our "wings" final examinations. Fred was absolutely hopeless at Morse Code and Aldis Lamp (in fact few of our flight were competent with the lamp) and where a certain standard had to be attained, I did all his examinations for him. When the results were announced in both subjects, he received more marks than me – there is no justice!

On the other side of the aerodrome, were based units of the American Air Force, flying mainly DC3s (Dakotas) on the 'Alaskan Highway', which starts at Edmonton, and was the trading route through to Alaska. I am probably the only person trained at Edmonton who did not have his photograph taken standing under the sign, eating a Banana, stating "This is the start of the Alaska Highway". We understood from the locals that RAF personnel were much preferred to the Americans, which was in sharp contrast to the situation which awaited us on our return to England!

Perhaps the fact that we were on Canadian Air Force rates of pay, enabled us to compete much more easily. A final memory of our meetings with the Americans were the races, side by side down the main highway to the aerodrome, as we returned to camp in our respective coaches at the end of an evening in town. I shall never know why there were no accidents.

On a personal note, Margaret and I became much closer, and spent all our time together when my duties and her work permitted. Nearly every weekend at the farm, walking the fields, feeding the animals, watching the milking of the cows, and even feeding the men in the fields when harvest time came. My favourite animals were the giant but docile Clydesdale carthorses. There were no motorised appliances available then. A particularly memory was a visit one Sunday to a small town, St Albert, which had remained very much as it was years before, and where there was the oldest Church in the West, still intact as when it was originally built, protected by its own wooden building, and containing all the memorabilia of the old West.

The "wings" ceremony, held in one of the main hangars, was most impressive with a Royal Canadian Air Force Band in attendance, and the awards made by a senior RCAF officer. At these ceremonies, guests were able to attend, but regrettably Margaret, due to office commitments was not able to be there. Always, the band, at some time during the ceremony played "Stardust", and this tune will always remind me of that special occasion.

No leave was granted, and so after one more day in Edmonton, which included a final nostalgic visit to the farm, and sorrowful farewells to my new friends including and especially Margaret, we had to catch the train to depart for Moncton and home. At least on this occasion we travelled as an ordinary passenger, and not in troop trains as on the outward journey. One of the many tunes of the day was Can This Be You Feeling Blue and, believe me, the answer was "YES". To say that I was full of regrets would be an understatement! It had been a wonderful six months, where I had gained my wings established a relationship, which would be a lasting memory (though sadly not continued after my stay in Germany). But it was a case of 'duty must come first'.

Our return journey to Moncton took four days travelling via Winnipeg and Montreal, but unfortunately did not allow us enough time for any extensive sightseeing.

Returning to the UK

Returning to Moncton was rather an anticlimax, but at least is was easy to separate the new arrivals from the old hands, who refused to wear greatcoats despite the cold weather, so their new wings were not covered. After a short stay of only a few days, we were moved by train to Halifax Nova Scotia, where we embarked on the SS Mauritania, to be told that we were the Security Guard on the voyage to the UK and home. The main body of passengers were American GIs on their way to England in anticipation of the second front. The vessel was absolutely packed with them, and by the time we sailed there was not very much room to move freely. We were warned that under no circumstances should we attempt to gamble with the Americans as there were many professionals among them.

On this return journey I was lucky on two counts, the first being a very smooth crossing with hardly a ripple to be seen in the Atlantic Ocean, although most of the way we travelled in thick fog. Some four days out from Halifax, it made our RAF contingent very happy and proud when a Sunderland Flying Boat appeared out of this gloom. It was encouraging to know that we were being watched over, against the menace of submarines. All of these cruise liners travelled under their own steam and unescorted. The second plus was encountering some of the regular Army who were manning the guns on the ship as permanent crew members, and they invited me to join them in their quarters, which were much more comfortable than the main deck where I had been housed.

This uneventful journey ended in Liverpool (Mauritania's home port) on Armistice day 1943, where we disembarked, and after much waiting about including custom's clearance, for our train, we eventually disembarked and arrived at our new destination – Harrogate – another transit camp. What did the future hold in store? We should soon know!

| CHAPTER 5 |

Joining Bomber Command

The wheels of the Royal Air Force organisation took over, we were sent on leave for two weeks, which was extended to three, and having arrived back in Harrogate we were soon to learn that most of us were destined for Bomber Command, and as the weeks passed by, the path to this end enfolded. Again this was a very pleasant period, and Harrogate was then still a delightful Spa town, and even during wartime it had a lot to offer.

There were many veterans from the Squadrons based in Yorkshire and in close proximity, who spent their days and weekends off in the town, adding a feeling which became common to us all when we ourselves were actually on a squadron. The work was hard but enjoyable, with advanced training in all aspects of our potential careers proceeding, but with some sport available, which was not surprising as our C/O was Leslie Ames, the Kent and England wicket keeper, with Sam Bartram the England goalkeeper and George Ainsly the Leeds soccer forward as PTIs. None of us ever played a game for the station team! I wonder why?

And where to next? Whitley Bay on the North East Coast on a Commando Course! Somehow I had never imagined myself as a Commando, but obviously the RAF did. This was a very vigorous period of training in all aspects of rifle drill, grenade throwing, field exercises, which I have no doubt did us a power of good, but we certainly did not appreciate it at the time. We never completed the course!

Right in the middle a posting came through for some of us to report to RAF Mona, which we found out was situated in the middle of the Isle of Anglesey, and was our Advanced Training School, would the war have finished sooner if I and my comrades had finished our Commando Course? We shall never know.

RAF Mona No. 8 Advanced Training School

We arrived at our new station in mid January 1944 after the usual war time cross country journey by train, to face for most of us our first experience of flying in home conditions. After the clear blue skies of Canada, it came as a nasty shock to the system, to find that as long as the cloud base was a minimum of 1,000 ft then flying would proceed. With the Irish Sea on two sides of us and the Welsh mountains behind us, it was not a comforting thought, and for the whole time that the course lasted, the cloud base never seemed to rise appreciably. The mountains, although only some six miles away could rarely be seen from the airfield, although they looked very beautiful from the air.

Again this was a compressed course, and most days and or nights we flew at least twice, covering the area down to Fishguard in the South, and over to Belfast and Barrow in the North and West, each flight being of two to three hours duration. Due to a miscalculation on one occasion, one of our aircraft flew over Dublin, which we understand did not please the natives, who were in a neutral country, and did nothing for the career of the Navigator in question, who was dismissed from the service.

Before I joined the RAF I had lost quite a few friends who had been fliers, plus those with whom I had nearly joined the Army pre-war, but an incident during the course brought home to me more clearly than any other the tragedies of war. I had flown in the morning on a usual training flight in one of our Ansons, a most dependable and safe Aircraft and that very afternoon, this same aircraft crashed soon after take off with all on board killed, including the Navigator, who had been with me all the time during our training in Canada and since. A very sad and traumatic experience.

It was here at Mona that I first met Ken Webb, a Wireless Operator/Air Gunner who had served in the Middle East as a ground operator, and subsequently re-mustered to Air Crew. The son of Charles Webb the Manager of Brighton Football Club, a well known character in the pre-war soccer world. Ken had been a reporter on his local Brighton newspaper until he enlisted in the RAF soon after war was declared, was married with a small daughter, and he and I soon became well acquainted and a firm friendship developed. It should be noted that RAF Mona was an advanced unit for the training of Navigators and Wop/AG's in parallel under qualified instructors, who in most cases were tour expired Air Crew on their rest period from operational flying, this being the policy throughout Training Command. As a result of our friendship, Ken and I agreed to become crew members, if we were posted to the same Operational Unit. We were!

Despite the deplorable weather conditions, including thick snow, which had to be cleared from the runways, flying continued with very little interruption, and very fortunately with no further accidents. The Meteorological forecasts before each of our flights became quite hilarious on most occasions, mainly because of the Pilots' refusal to believe that any decent weather ever approached Anglesey, but this did not stop our training programme proceeding. On one occasion, we had just left dense cloud and arrived in clear skies, right over the middle of a convoy forming in the Irish Sea near to the entrance to Liverpool docks, and as we reached the end, we were recalled to base because of bad weather, and had to turn right round and fly right back over the convoy. The Navy were kind to us on this occasion. There was no friendly flak. At a later briefing, my name was not on the flying order, and it was rather a shock when I was designated to navigate the Wing Commander Flying to Barrow on a special trip. This was quite uneventful, and on reflection, and in view of later experience, I do not really think he required me at all to navigate. Such is fame!

Our off duty evenings and other spare time was spent in the local village of Llangefni, or if time allowed in the delightful town of Bangor, where we found that the local population were not always as friendly as one would expect. Time did not allow for any detailed examination of the local countryside, and it was many years later before this was rectified. This course of some six weeks duration, eventually came to an end, and with the announcement that our next step would be Operational Training Unit, where our training would continue towards our ultimate destination, an operational Squadron in Bomber Command. In my case this was to be RAF Wymeswold, near

Loughborough, and it was good to know that my new found friend Ken Webb, was also on the same posting.

Operational Training Unit No. 28

This was the start of the really serious side of our training, being the run-up to the commencement of our operational flying. Conditions and activities were all geared to providing replacements in the Squadron for those crews fortunate enough to complete their tours (first 30 trips and after a rest period a second and final 20 trips), and other less fortunate crews who did not complete, either being killed, wounded or taken prisoner of war. Some individuals went on to complete more than the designated two tours, but once the statutory two tours had been completed, there was no compulsion to continue operational flying. At this time, the Battle of Berlin was at its height, with casualties as high or even higher than at any time during the war.

In the peculiar custom known only to the Royal Air Force, it was here that crews were formed from those arriving from the various advanced flying schools in categories of Pilot, Navigator, Bomb Aimer, Wireless Operator/Air Gunner, and Air Gunners. This was a purely voluntary arrangement in accordance with a force which in all cases consisted of volunteers. I had already agreed to fly with Ken Webb but you can well imagine my surprise, when at our first gathering I met again John Austin, who had joined up and travelled with me to Air Crew Recruitment Centre at Lords Cricket Ground, some two years previously. He had now qualified as a pilot and it did not take long to decide that John should be our Pilot, and we soon added Norman Osman (Ossy) as our Bomb Aimer. This only left us with two Air Gunners to find and we decided on Frank Wright, who was from Bury, and Brian Hamilton (Blondie), whose father was a Warrant Officer in the RAF of many years standing. They had trained together at Gunnery School, had become good friends and decided to fly together. They were both just 18 years of age.

And so our crew was formed:

Pilot: John Austin from Luton, age 20

Navigator: Philip Potts from Luton, age 21

Bomb Aimer: Ossy Osman from Harrow, age 22

WoP/AG: Ken Webb from Brighton, age 26

M/U Gunner: Frank Wright from Bury, age 18

Rear Gunner: Blondie Hamilton from Cannock, age 18

An operational crew consisted of seven members, but it was normal practice for the Flight Engineer to join a crew at Heavy Bomber Conversion Unit at a later date.

Despite the fact that we all considered ourselves quite experienced, it came as quite a shock to find that our first few weeks were spent on ground training. In fact, we did virtually no flying during this period, but concentrated very hard on advanced techniques, which in my own case was devoted to Navigation, particularly my first introduction to Radar in the form of the "Gee Box" a navigational aid. Not only were we instructed in the latest flying and Navigational aids, but survival in case of our aircraft's sudden demise, was also high on the curriculum, and this included procedures for abandoning aircraft on crash landing, ditching in the sea, and what to do in case of fire (a lesson later on which we appreciated).

Who can forget 'dinghy drill' in the swimming pool of Loughborough College? Arriving by the side of the pool, completely naked, we were instructed to put on Mae Wests (sopping wet from the previous victims) and to climb to the highest point of the diving board, jump into the water, swim to the dinghy in an upturned position at the furthest point of the pool, turn it over and climb in. Not as easy as it looked, particularly for a non swimmer like Ken, who was towed with much glugging and spluttering by the two gunners, and unceremoniously tipped over the side. We were advised that it would not be as easy as this if we had to ditch in the cold unfriendly wastes of the North Sea. Basic parachute drill was given in the gymnasium, and consisted of verbal instruction only, and a practice jump to show landing procedures, not from a static tower, but from the top of a climbing tower frame. I understand that this was the most any in Bomber Command received, and some not even that. Their first practice was when they were shot down, and forced to jump!

Our off duty time during this period was mainly spent in Loughborough, where I became friendly with a local Air Training Corp Officer, and in fact did a certain amount of lecturing to his cadets. As a crew we were very quickly becoming firm friends, and as happened with most crews became almost inseparable and spent most of our off duty time together. The satellite aerodrome for Wymeswold was Castle Donnington (now East Midlands Airport) and for the flying portion of our training we were transferred there, and introduced to the Wellington Bomber, a stalwart of Bomber Command since the beginning of the war, and as we discovered for ourselves, a much loved aircraft, with virtually no vices. We did find one vice, which on the first occasion came as a nasty surprise, but on the second cost us dearly. As we taxied towards the runway to take off, we noticed our Engineering Officer chasing our aircraft around the perimeter track in his car, in a state of extreme wrath. When eventually he caught up with us he fined us on the spot the sum of ten shillings (quite a lot in those days). Our crime was to have omitted to ensure that the twin hatches above the pilots were closed and properly bolted in position. This would cause them to fly open on takeoff, and despite all efforts they were impossible to close once the plane was airborne.

After the Preliminary familiarisation flights to accustom ourselves to this new aircraft, vastly different from the Ansons previously flown, we soon embarked on a series of cross country and other exercises including practice bombing on the ranges. Whereas previously we had only flown a duration of some two to three hours in Ansons, we were now regularly flying in excess of six hours on every trip.

Looking back in my log book, it can be seen that in these "cross countries" we covered nearly all parts of the British Isles, excluding Ireland, but two trips in particular stand out in my memory. One night flight, we spent the whole of our time in the air sandwiched between two sets of clouds. Our aircraft could not climb above 15,000ft and we were unable to obtain any wireless fixes, nor did we carry any radar devices. We saw the ground just once through the clouds. Navigation was carried out using 'dead reckoning' only, and on return to base the Navigation Leader complimented me but also remarked that some people are lucky and that someone 'up there' must have been guiding me!

On another occasion in daylight, just prior to D-Day, we were on a trip down through the centre of England and then over to the West Country, when, with very ominous Cumulo Nimbus clouds approaching, our port engine developed a very serious oil leak, and we had to take the decision to land as soon as possible. Below us were innumerable aerodromes, but none were marked on my plotting maps, and so for the one and only time, we had to use the 'darky' procedure to obtain permission to land. This procedure was introduced to help aircraft in distress, and would only answer calls from aircraft using the exact set wording. On landing we found we were on an aerodrome predominately for and with gliders, in fact we were right in the middle of a whole complex of aerodromes training for the great day. For the record (and my own ego), we were only one mile off the track we should have been on!

In addition to the flying, the usual ground classes all combined to make us fit and competent for the more arduous tasks to follow on completion of our operational training.

Our off duty moments, which were now seriously curtailed, due to spending much more time in the air both by day and night, were spent in the local village of Castle Donnington, with the occasional trip to Long Eaton and even on one occasion to Derby. Although mainly devoted to scouring the local pubs, some time was found for my favourite hobby of dancing in the local halls.

This course culminated in our first trip over foreign territory, being a leaflet dropping exercise over France to Blois, known as a operation 'Nickel', with a duration of just over six hours. It was with a great sigh of relief and of satisfaction when we returned and landed quite safely. As we crossed the French coast we had taken a photograph, as instructed, but little did we know at the time that this would be the area where the landings would be when the D-Day operation began, or that this would herald our demise in Bomber Command.

Upon completion we were rated an "above average" crew, and I personally was graded "above average" with a recommendation to become an instructor after more experience (i.e. after I completed my first tour).

By this time we had become part of the well oiled machinery of Bomber Command training, and after a short leave, during which all the crew attended our Bomb Aimer's wedding at Harrow, we were posted to our next stage.

No. 1656 Heavy Bomber Conversion Unit, Lindholme

This was our introduction to four-engined bombers, in the form of the Handley-Page Halifax, again a most delightful aircraft, to which our skipper Johnnie soon became accustomed. We also gained our Flight Engineer, Fred, an ex-policeman from Harrow. Virtually our only activity here was flying on cross-country exercises and dummy bombing raids on large targets such as Newcastle, known as "Command Exercises" again with duration in excess of six hours. After each flight, great care was taken in the examination of logs and charts to ensure that no major mistakes were being made in application, always bearing in mind that in the very near future, trips would not be over the friendly home countries but over most unfriendly enemy territory. Our off-duty was much restricted, but any we had was spent in Doncaster or Sheffield.

During this training period, we awoke on the 6 June 1944 to the announcement of the opening of the second front, a very well kept secret of which we had no prior knowledge whatsoever.

Our final hurdle before reaching an operational squadron was imminent.

No. 1 Lancaster Finishing School, Hemswell

This was exactly what it said, a very brief two week course, in which we converted from the Halifax to the Avro Lancaster four-engined bomber. I shall never forget our first familiarisation flight, with Johnnie at the controls, when our tutor took us down to 1,000 ft over Lincolnshire and instructed him to feather (stop) two engines on the same wing, reduce speed on one engine on the other wing, and then to start climbing. None of us on board thought this possible, but our Lancaster (a well-used one you will understand) responded nobly, and although the rate was not high, we climbed. From this point onwards we never doubted the ability of the Lancaster.

We had now, so we thought, completed our training, and we were ready to take our place in a squadron, which we were informed would be No 103, Elsham Wolds, wherever that might be.

| CHAPTER 6 |

Operations

No. 103 Squadron, 1 Group, Elsham Wolds

We found that Elsham was in North Lincolnshire, near the village of Barnetby, some half way between Scunthorpe and Grimsby, which was the railway station used by the camp for incoming Air Crew. Upon arrival we were introduced as a crew to our Squadron Commander, Wg/Cdr St John, by the adjutant, who after interviewing us and reading our training notes advised us that we would be in "A" Flight led by Flt/Lt Van Rolleghan, a Belgian who was the flight commander.

But did we start operating immediately? – We did not!

Our new Squadron did not trust training command, and we were informed that we must do several extensive cross country training exercises before we were accepted, with the added threat that if we did not reach the required standard we would be returned to training command. We had hardly started, when our own and our sister Squadron No. 576 took a severe hammering on a trip to Stuttgart, with the loss of many aircraft and damage to nearly all others. As it was impossible to prepare sufficient aircraft for operations, all flying personnel, including my own crew, were sent on seven days leave. Little did I know that this would be my last leave for some considerable time, or in fact the last leave ever for Johnnie, Ken and Blondie.

After returning from leave, all aircraft having been repaired or replaced while we were away, we began our very short life as members of the squadron by doing the cross countries designated by our Flight Commander to ensure that we met with their standards. In accordance with usual practice, our skipper was sent on an operation as second pilot to familiarise him, and on another operation Frank went on an operation as a spare Gunner with another crew. Fortunately both returned unharmed and very much more knowledgeable about the unknown.

As a crew we then commenced our operational tour, though it turned out to be very short lived. Our first op was to France, over the Normandy landing area where allied forces were closing the Falaise Gap, and Bomber Command had been called in to assist. When we arrived at flights for this our first trip, we found to our consternation that our designated aircraft had fitters crawling over the rear wing, repairing one of the fins. When we queried our safety, the Engineering Officer cheerfully advised that should it come off while we were away, it would be easier for the control Tower to recognise our aircraft! We did return, and for our next trip went on a daylight raid into Belgium and Holland attacking aerodromes, accompanied by the 8th American Air Force, which was causing much damage right into Germany itself. Our own target was Le Culot, where we were instructed to not only aim for the buildings but just as importantly the runways.

This was followed a day later with a long haul to Stettin at night, returning with almost nine hours in our log books. Our route had taken us close to the coast of Norway, and as we made our way over the Skagerrak we could see the lights of Sweden clearly below us.

Without our knowledge and with no redress, just two days later, our crew, along with several others in the Group, was accused of bombing short and onto our own troops on our trip to the Falaise Gap.

We had been aware that we were only bombing 400 yards in front of our own troops, but deemed it impossible that we should be accused as we had been called down by the 'master bomber' to 5,000ft and were in the middle of a most appalling column of smoke when we dropped our bombs.

However, you cannot argue with decisions made by higher authority in the Royal Air Force. As a penance, we were instructed to make a special attack on a Flying Bomb site in France.

On the 18th August 1944, with the other crews similarly accused (16 all told) we were briefed to bomb in daylight, flying bomb launch sites in the Pas de Calais area of France. At that time, the Germans were still using these weapons to attack targets in England. We were briefed to bomb at 10,000ft, our target La Nieppe. A fighter escort would meet us as we left the English coast, and there would be light cloud only. At our own discretion only we could bomb below 10,000ft, but the fighters would be there to protect us. This did not turn out to be the case. By the time we reached the French coast, no fighter cover had arrived, and we were in 10/10th cloud. The crew, initiated by our skipper (we were very inexperienced) decided to go in and bomb below cloud, and I, as Navigator, plotted us in to the target. As we came out of the cloud at approximately 5,000ft the target was dead ahead and the Bomb Aimer took over. Unfortunately, so did the light anti-aircraft batteries surrounding the Flying Bomb sites and we were hit very badly in the early stages of our bombing run. Very quickly the starboard inner engine was a raging inferno, and a second burst came through the underside of the aircraft, killing the Wop/AG (Ken) outright and taking out most of my plotting table, leaving a nasty hole in the roof above my head. Despite this we completed our bombing run, dropped our bombs and took our photograph – but all to no avail. It was obvious that we could not continue to fly. Had it simply been the engine on fire we may have been able to douse it, but by this time the whole of the wing inboard of the engine was ablaze. The skipper gave the order to bale out while he could still control the aircraft. All crew members acknowledged this order, and proceeded forward to evacuate through the front hatch. The order of exit was first the Bomb Aimer, who removed the hatch as he was already in the nose, second the Flight Engineer who was standing next to the Pilot and third the Navigator. As third man out, I waited until the Mid Upper Gunner appeared over the main spar, having already announced that Ken had been killed, and then jumped through the hatch. The evacuation had been carried out strictly in accordance with exercises we had performed on many occasions, with all crew members having acknowledged compliance with the skipper's order to bale out. It therefore came as a great surprise that no further parachutes appeared for some time after I had jumped. I was already floating down in mine, having left the aircraft at about 3,000ft. Finally, one more left the aircraft, but at a much lower level, meaning that there were still two men on board.

By this time the ground was approaching very rapidly, and the aircraft had circled below and underneath me, seemingly in an attempt to make a crash landing. I had to side-slip my parachute to avoid landing on or near the aircraft, but to my horror before it reached the ground it exploded in a mass of flames, with ammunition exploding in all directions. It was obvious that nothing could be done for the two men still on board, but why had they not jumped?

Not until I met Frank, our Mid-Upper Gunner, some time later, did I receive any sort of explanation.

When he reached the Flight Engineer's position he replugged into the intercom system, to hear the skipper talking to Blondie, who was still in the rear turret, which surprised him as he thought that he had already left his position. The skipper insisted that Frank jumped, and helped him on his way with his foot. By this time the aircraft had lost considerable height. In the years since, Frank and I have discussed this on many occasions, but to this day we do not know what happened or why they stayed in the aircraft. I can only make the assumption that Blondie was trapped and the skipper tried in vain to crash land the plane rather than bale out and leave him to die...

By the time I reached the ground, making a perfect landing – head, bottom and heels (though not at all in accordance with the manual) my mind was in turmoil, trying to remember all the instructions given to us, as to what to do if and when we were shot down. Strangely, looking back over the years, I do not remember being afraid during the action, and as I recall, there was nothing very brave about jumping out of a burning aircraft to save one's own life – self preservation is a great instinct.

Being on enemy territory in a strange land, however, was a vastly different proposition. I had a very good idea where I was. I should have done anyway, after all I was the Navigator and we were shot down over the target! But what to do? Even though it was 10 o'clock at night, it was still light and would be for a further one or two hours. This part of France, the Pas de Calais, despite the fact that allied troops were by now advancing in all directions from their landing zones, was – according to reports – still absolutely crawling with Germans, due to the proximity of the Channel ports, the flying bomb sites and the flak batteries.

Within a few minutes of landing, I was met by a French girl, who quickly gathered up my parachute, and ran off in the direction whence she had come, whilst at the same time pointing for me to head in the opposite direction. Not having completely gathered myself together, I followed her directions and found a small ditch in which I though I could hide in until darkness came. But to no avail! Within a very short time I was surrounded by German troops, one carrying the largest hand weapon I had ever seen. I subsequently found out they were in the Lufftwaffe, and manning the local flak batteries. Of the eight Aircraft who had decided to attempt to bomb our target, two were shot down and [at a later date I was advised] that all the others had been damaged to some degree.

A few days after I had been shot down, I was able to swap experiences with a pilot who had been downed on the same raid, and he told me he had spent his first night sheltering under a hedge, while overhead flying bombs were beginning their deadly missions.

W found out later that the other eight aircraft involved had turned back at the French coast. Perhaps in hindsight that was the wisest thing to have done... and we never did find out what happened to our fighter escort!

| CHAPTER 7 |

Capture and Incarceration

After being captured I was taken to a building in the vicinity where I spent the night in a dark room below ground level with a concrete floor, no light, no bedding or any form of furniture and certainly no home comforts. Trying to get some sleep in these conditions, as can be imagined, was rather difficult. My cigarettes, matches and watch had been taken from me, and all I had were my thoughts! What was to happen next? I had never done anything like this before and could only pray that this was not the end of everything.

The next few days passed and I have only faint recollections of events, but do remember being moved on several occasions by truck, and have a vivid memory of spending a night in a cell in Lille. In the morning we were lined up in a yard (by this time there were three or four of us captured airmen) with a line of men who looked like labourers of some sort who were all carrying forks and spades. As can be imagined we feared the worst, but fortunately they went off in one direction and we in another!

Eventually I arrived by train in Brussels, where we found our destination was the castle, which had been turned into an interrogation centre for captured allied airmen. The cell block remains clearly in my mind, a line of cells, each containing one prisoner, and apart from a bed and one dirty blanket, nothing else, but a small barred window too high to reach. There was a signalling arm which could be activated by the inmates to indicate to the guard that you required to use the toilet. We soon found that toilet paper was severely rationed, approximately three sheets per person, but with the low intake of food (tasteless thin soup and black bread) this was not much of a hardship. We found out later, in other camps, that this was in fact luxury! To amuse ourselves we used to take it in turns to signal to the guards, much to their annoyance and this became our first experience of 'Goon baiting'.

Periodically we were taken (individually) from our cells for interrogation by German Officers of varying rank, but by this stage in the war this was not carried out in any great depth. They mainly seemed to want details of our targets: somewhat pointless considering we had been shot down in the process of bombing them, which to us appeared to be fairly conclusive evidence! As mentioned earlier, food was hardly a priority during this period of our captivity, but the daily ration supplied consisting of thin soup, black bread, ertsatz coffee, and no cigarettes, was only a foretaste of what was to become our staple diet until the end of the war.

After a period of some 3 - 4 days we heard a sound, which in time would become very familiar: "Raus Raus!" It meant that some inmates, including myself, were on the move. We were placed on a train at Brussels station for we knew not where. Our only comfort was when a curtain in an upper window at the station parted and someone, presumably Belgian, quickly but unmistakably made the "V" for victory sign. We found that our destination was Oberursel, just outside Frankfurt, where we arrived at "Dulag Luft" which was the main interrogation centre for captured allied airmen. It was here that many forms were brought to us in our solitary cells, with requests that they should be completed on the grounds that they were required by the International Red Cross for the benefit of our families. The only genuine item I recognised on these forms, was in fact the Red Cross in the corner of the document, and really it was our introduction to the 'ferrets' whom we encountered when we reached our designated camp. These 'ferrets' were Germans, usually speaking English with an American accent, who roamed the compounds seeking information from the prisoners.

Despite the pressures imposed on us by these, plus several interviews with senior German Officers, who without exception spoke perfect English and boasted of their love of England, few people gave more than they were required to by the Geneva Convention (i.e. Name, Rank and Number).

This was a particularly harrowing time, as we were completely isolated from our comrades, with no sight of a friendly face and the discomfort of not knowing what was going to happen next, or how long the ordeal was going to last. But there is always an ending, for better or worse, and after a few days I was transferred to the main compound where I could mingle with my comrades, who included my own Bomb Aimer, Ossy, and at least we could exchange experiences.

Our next destination was the transit camp at Wetzler, a few kilometres north of Frankfurt, where we were given a Red Cross case, which contained essential domestic kit, and had a hot shower, in my own case the first since I had been shot down some 10-14 days previously. From here we would be transferred to whichever prisoner of war camp we were designated, and it was here that I broke the unwritten law of "never volunteer".

There was a vacancy in the cookhouse, and this was an opportunity I could not miss. The food was a slight improvement on that received previously, but this was entirely due to the supplementation of the German ration by the Red Cross parcels, which were now available. By now it was late August, and it was also the wasp season and in the Mess Hall we were absolutely inundated with them. As jam was a popular item in Red Cross parcels, many a contest was held to see who could catch the most. I remember that on the wall of the mess were several drawings in cartoon fashion, made by a very talented artist, showing evasive action taken by the men while trying to enjoy their meal. But this apparent high life could not last, and after a stay of approximately 10 days, which with hindsight I found had been luxury compared with what was to come, a consignment of some 20 of us were entrained for our new home: Stalag Luft 7, in Bankau, Upper Silesia (wherever that might be). It turned out to be part of Poland, and it soon appeared on the horizon, as we found ourselves some 100 miles south east of Breslau with Sagan a well established camp, virtually in a direct line in a north-easterly direction. At that time Sagan was merely a name, and the diabolical events of some months earlier (50 RAF officers killed after escaping) had not yet filtered through to us. Very late in the evening, after a train ride (on this occasion in carriages and not horse wagons) in which we travelled all the way across Germany, including a brief glimpse of the River Rhine, we arrived at the local station which was approximately two miles from the camp, and our new adventure began.

Stalag Luft 7, Bankau, Upper Silesia

Our party of new inmates was marched into the outer compound, where the usual formalities (with which we were now becoming accustomed) took place: searches, documentation, counting, finger printing and anything else the Germans considered necessary to ensure that we were easily identified if trying to escape – prior to us being allowed into the main compound. I became Kriegsfangener (prisoner of war) No. 719 – a 'kregie' as it was shortened by the inmates. Waiting inside the wire by the main gate was a collection of those who had already arrived, including my own Mid Upper gunner, Frank, all seeking familiar faces, and the cries of greetings as old colleagues met again echoed round the compound. We were soon advised that this was a new camp, especially prepared for allied Air Force personnel, in an area of Upper Silesia which was considered to be escape-proof. We were to be housed in the temporary accommodation provided in a small area next to the main camp, which was still under construction. Known as the 'rabbit hutches' because of their size, each housed some 10-12 persons, and had no lights, no cooking facilities, and our latrine was an open pit where one had to balance on a round pole, which received each day a plentiful supply of lime, the smell of which was with us at all times.

Finding our feet in these new surroundings was our first priority, and here my earlier training in the Scouts became most valuable. Added to this were the engineering skills of my Bomb Aimer Ossy, who was with me, and became most adept at tin bashing (the conversion of tins from the Red Cross parcels) into eating and cooking utensils, an essential feature if you wanted to eat. Frank had arrived at the camp earlier than Ossy and I, and although we saw him daily, he had already joined another 'compound' (the term used for a collection of people who had agreed to eat/work together). I should also mention at this stage that our Flight Engineer on our final mission was unknown to us as he was only flying with us as a substitution for our own Engineer, who was unable to fly. For this reason there is little mention of him in this narrative, the only known fact was that on his last trip with his previous crew, he had to 'bale out' and had broken his ankle on landing and this had been his first trip since recovering. He too had arrived at a different time and had joined another 'compound'. He had probably seen enough of us anyway!

The routine of camp life soon became familiar to us. Morning and afternoon we had 'Appel' (parades), usually under the supervision of the Camp Commandant, an obvious survivor of World War I, an upright grey-haired officer, immaculate in his field grey uniform, and obviously not of the Nazi school, with Ober Fieldwebel Franks, another survivor of WWI in charge of the parade. He was the typical German soldier we had read about in our history books, whose shout caused more alarm in his own ranks than it did in ours, but he was always scrupulously fair in his treatment of kriegies. On one occasion after 'Goon baiting' had reached quite alarming proportions he was heard to say "Good Soldiers, Bad Prisoners!" Needless to say we considered this a compliment!

A daily walk around the compound, always anticlockwise and usually in pairs was known as 'circuit bashing' and was almost mandatory. Then there was the collection of the daily ration from the kitchen, receiving Red Cross parcels (on a weekly basis at first and invariably thereafter two persons per parcel) and bartering with those who did not smoke or eat chocolate. There were few of the latter and those who craved a cigarette found it was stronger than their hunger. For our inconvenience, apart from the guards on the outside of the wire and those in the watch towers (I am sure most readers will have a good idea of the layout of a camp with its barbed wire, trip wire, watch tower and searchlights) there were the guards in the camp who we called 'goons' watching our every movement. More importantly, inside the compound was another species of German known as "ferrets". Most of these spoke English, often with a pronounced American accent, and all tried to ingratiate themselves with the inmates in an endeavour to obtain information about possible escape plans etc. These 'ferrets', once identified, were used, of course, for our own ends, whenever possible.

One of our biggest problems was obtaining firewood for our fires (as none was supplied) which had to be made outside in true camping style, much to the annoyance of the guards, particularly when they tripped in the holes made for this purpose, while on night duty, or trying to contain a dog on a leash.

Mostly our huts suffered for this purpose, and by the time we were moved into our new quarters in the main compound, most had been stripped so severely of supporting timbers, that it was a miracle that they had stayed up at all. In fact, one hut totally collapsed when somebody leaned on it too heavily! Light was provided by making candles by melting cooking grease into small tins from the Red Cross parcels, and using strands carefully extracted from various garments as wicks. One compensation for us during this period was the incredible weather, with a hot sun blazing down every day from morning until night.

We were moved to our new accommodation at the end of September 1944. Each barrack block was of wooden construction, raised on blocks, so that there was a gap of approximately three feet of clear space underneath as a deterrent against possible escapes. There were eight blocks, plus two toilet blocks, an administration building, and a kitchen and storehouse. The blocks consisted of fourteen rooms, with a small utility room at one end available for use by all inhabitants, with a central corridor. Each room was intended to house twelve persons, sleeping in double bunks, complete with a wooden table and a small heating stove. This was soon revised when the a large intake of glider pilots arrived at the end of September/ early October after the debacle at Arnhem. You may ask why, when we were an all Royal Air Force and Allied Air Force camp previous to this, how Glider Pilots (part of the Army) were allowed in. We could only presume that, as they were wearing 'wings', the Germans could not tell the difference!

It was in room seven that I first met Jim Davies, who became my constant companion on the circuits, and one of the few kreigies with whom good conversation was possible. Jim had arrived in the camp just before me, but unlike me he had been shot down several months previously and along with his Bomb Aimer, Ron Aiken, he had spent six months with the Dutch resistance in Northern Holland. They were on an escape route through Holland and Belgium, but due to a breakdown in the line, they ended in Gestapo Headquarters in Antwerp in early August 1944. After interrogation by the Gestapo he wound up in Bankau – but it was not until we moved into the main compound that I actually met with him. Although he never mentioned the names of those who had helped him, he acknowledged to me the great debt he owed them.

Fortunately most of those brave people survived the war, and this was fully appreciated when Jim's book A Leap in the Dark was published in early 1994 which gave a detailed account of his time with them, their efforts on his behalf to return him safely to England, his subsequent capture in Antwerp, and his days in the POW camp.

During our many conversations we discussed our career prospects. He was already a trainee schoolteacher, and it came as no surprise to me, when we eventually met many years after the war had ended, that having had a successful career following his chosen profession, he became the Principal of a college in Bangor, North Wales.

When transferred into the main camp, I with Ossy were housed in room No. 7 Barrack Block 8, and interestingly in rooms 1 and 13 were kreigies of long standing, who had been guests of the Germans for several years. This was highlighted on Appel one morning when a very tall, good looking immaculately dressed young German Officer took the parade, and when seeing some familiar faces in the ranks of block 8, approached, and with a large smile, called out "Get up them bloody stairs", much to the amazement of most of us standing there. We learnt afterwards that he had been in a previous camp with some of our old lags, who had taught him several English phrases including the above. Apparently this was the only English he knew.

Our daily life assumed a recognised pattern, with morning appel starting our daily routine, followed by all or any activities that were available to us. In the new compound we had more scope for our sporting activities, initially starting with cricket and as winter approached, football and rugby. For the more academic there were classes started, but being a new camp there were no textbooks available, and any subjects taught were conducted verbally and in the main concentrated on German and French languages. Added to this were lectures given by various people, and two of them remain in my memory given by the CoE Padre and one by the Medical Officer. Every Sunday morning services for all denominations were held, and were always well attended.

Food tended to dominate our every thought and conversation, and although most of us were relatively fit on arrival, there is no doubt that it was only the addition of the Red Cross parcels to supplement the German rations (which were not sufficient to sustain us), that maintained us in a reasonable condition.

Considering that before we were shot down most of us smoked and drank too much, the fact that we had nothing to drink at all of the intoxicating variety and a very restricted supply of cigarettes, was in fact a benefit, although we did not appreciate it at the time! Red Cross parcels were received from the UK, Canada and the USA and depending on their origin, contained supplies of tinned foods, butter, spreads, chocolate and cigarettes. They were intended as one parcel per person, and it was very rarely that the issue rose above one parcel per two persons and very often more. In all rooms the 'compound' system was in operation for messing purposes, and this could range from two persons or, as in many cases (including my own) the whole room. In any case one person had to be nominated to collect the German rations from the kitchen, usually daily at mid day. Many days was this delayed because of the sounding of the Air Raid siren heralding the arrival of the American Air Force, on one of their missions into SE Germany/ Poland.

After the evening appel, our nightly activities consisted mainly of card games, with Bridge dominating, although conversation was more prevalent at this period, with topics such as food, sex, but mostly stories of how people had been shot down, or any other harrowing experiences during their operational life. A highlight was the occasional opportunity to borrow the camp gramophone and records, always with the instruction to play the Harry James record once only during the evening, as apparently the high notes damaged the needles more than any other and these were in short supply. (Fact or fiction – who knows?)

It was also during the evening that a regular caller to every room, in our case Jock, one of the old lags from room one, read us the news from England, which he had listened to on our illegal radio. I never did know where this was hidden, but for all my time in camp, the news was regularly circulated to everybody, which made it very difficult to keep quiet when given conflicting information from established German news bulletins. Even at a later date when we were on our forced march, the news was still received. We did, of course, regularly listen to Lord Haw Haw by courtesy of the German broadcast system, but none of us took much notice of what he was saying.

During this period, until we were marched out of camp in mid January 1945 in the face of the advancing Russian Troops, the events which are imprinted on my mind are mainly:

1. The absolute luxury when we were permitted to have a hot shower, which was not often. The cold showers were available at all times, but as winter approached only the very hardy (and I was one believe it or not) took advantage of this facility.

2. The pot of water, which, in virtually every room was waiting on top of the stove, always ready to make a "brew". Circulation within the camp was permitted at all times, except during an air raid warning and during the hours between lights out and the morning.

3. The smell of a pipe smoking German guard. We subsequently found out from personal experience that this was the only thing to do with their issue of Mint Tea!

4. The anticipation when the call was made "Red Cross parcels up" – would it be English, Canadian, or American? What would we receive to "swap". Would we be smoking Players, Woodbines, Camels or Winchesters?

5. The boys in room 13 of our block, under the leadership of 'Snowy' Snowden. Who can forget the day they marched across the parade ground before being dismissed, went into the toilet block, and after an interval during which the German guards were having apoplectic fits, returned to their places as if nothing had happened!

6. The tunnel which was started from this same room, coinciding with the preparation they were also making for an ice skating rink, outside their window. Its anybody's guess what they intended to use as skates. Unfortunately neither were successful, which is not really surprising as one member of this room was a man by the name of Hughes, who arrived in the camp in October 1944, much better dressed than any of us, including brown leather gloves, and who after his return to this country after the war, was subsequently Court Martialled, tried and found guilty of collaboration with Germans, and sentenced to five years in prison.

7. The occasion when the German authorities decreed that the twelve men in the camp who were not NCOs were to be set to work, which is in accordance with the Geneva Convention. Reluctantly it was agreed that twelve men would work, but not necessarily the twelve in question. As you can imagine twelve of the most difficult Kreigies were chosen, and in a very short time mayhem reigned supreme. They were meant to erect a hut in a compound near the main gate, but at the end of a hard days work, this compound was full of holes (for foundations) and most of the hut had found its way into the main compound to be used for firewood! We never heard what happened to the guards in charge of the working party, but the experiment was never repeated.

8. The beautiful weather when we first arrived, lasting until the end of October, only broken by the November rains, leading into the crisp, cold air of December and January.

9. The constant air raid warnings, invariably somewhere about mid day when we regularly saw the American Air Force on their way to bomb the Oil Refineries in Romania. During this period an unfortunate incident occurred when a young Canadian Air Gunner, Les Stevenson, in our block went out of the hut before an "All Clear" was sounded in the camp, and was shot by a German Guard parading outside the wire, and died some hours later.

10. The camp concert given just before Christmas 1944, before we had to evacuate the camp for good. To sing "God Save the King" was forbidden by the Germans, but "Land of Hope and Glory" was its replacement, and sung with great gusto.

11. Christmas Day, when the Germans decreed that there would be no appels that day. The way in which every Kriegie tried to enjoy this day in their way. I played Football, representing England against Scotland, but do not remember who won, but who cared? We could hear German voices singing Carols in their own quarters, mostly we could not understand the words, but the tunes were identical to our own. There were some who had devised a 'still' to make spirits from the Raisins and Prunes from the Red Cross parcels, but I did not take part in this and from the look of those who did the next morning, it was a wise decision! However, it was inevitable that many a heavy heart was thinking of home, particularly those who were spending their second, third or even fourth year in captivity.

12. The meetings in our room of Jim and his Welsh speaking friends, I never did understand the language but well understood the need for these people who did to converse in their own tongue. This also applied to two Polish Airmen also in my room, whose bidding in English when playing Bridge, was almost as incomprehensive as their language.

13. The mad scrabble when the rumours that we were moving out in the face of the Russian advance became reality. Were we really going to go outside those gates at last? Eventually we did, but only after some delay, and the events of the three weeks after we left are forever imprinted on my mind, but that is another story.

And so our stay at Stalag Luft 7 ended, but who will forget the comradeship, the continuous fight in our own way against the enemy, and our desire to live and be free. As we left the gates of the camp the reality seemed much closer, but little did we know what was in store for us. Our trials and tribulations were still to come, we did not know then, but soon found out that our time in Stalag Luft 7 had been comparatively kind to us, with hardships that were at least bearable.

From:- The Rev. B.T.Croft, R.A.F.V.R.

R.A.F. STATION,
ELSHAM WOLDS. Lincs.

28th, August,1944.

Dear Mr. Potts,

May I, as your son's Padre, be allowed to express my deep sympathy with you and all who know and love him and assure you that our prayers here at the Station Church will be joined with yours for him and all who are missing.

I think you might like to know that at one of the Holy Communion services here during the week we regularly remember by name those churchmen who are posted missing.

I trust that in your anxiety at this time you will let your religion be a source of strength and comfort to you. It can be - as I myself and so many others have proved during these war years.

The power and peace of God which comes to us, especially through prayer and sacrament and the reading of our Bibles, enables the Christian to face anxiety and sorrow as men and women "not without hope".

Please let me know if I can be of any help to you or if you would like me to put your own parish priest into touch with you; at the same time, please do not feel that this letter demands any acknowledgement.

Yours very sincerely,

....
Church of England Chaplain.

Mr. E.Potts,
24, Napier Road,
LUTON.
Beds.

| CHAPTER 8 |

Forced March and Afterwards

Forced March – January 1945

By the end of our first night's march, the reality of our situation had turned to hard fact, that there was a long way ahead, and who knew what hardship we had to face. Most of us had loaded as many of our personal possessions into our Red Cross cases as possible, and fixed some sort of straps so that it could be more easily carried on our shoulders. It soon became obvious to a lot of us, that carrying unnecessary items such as books was not a good idea, and within the first few hours of leaving camp, the countryside was littered with unwanted equipment.

The story of the march (who said it was a march?) some 1,500 men straggled out over a considerable distance, most determinedly pressing on in the most deplorable conditions, in which we entailed snow, below freezing temperatures, very little food, and the most uncomfortable accommodation imaginable. Barns, cow sheds, and any other out building that could be found. Memories of this period of my life are etched vividly in my memory, although some detail is vague, but always will remain the endeavour of individual people in maintaining the moral of the marchers. In particular I remember our Padre, Rev. John Collins, a big man in every respect, who had rowed in winning crews for Cambridge in three successive Boat Races before the war, who endlessly went up and down the column encouraging and assisting in every way. Other memories or incidents remain in more detail.

On about the third day soon after passing through a typical German village, one of my colleagues asked if I would like a cup of milk. Would I like a cup of milk? What a silly question! I was convinced he was joking. However, as requested I trudged back down the column, and met with a closely bunched crowd, who were pushing an old pram, which contained a churn of milk, purloined, I subsequently found out, when they were passing a farm with its collecting platform outside. The most satisfying cup of milk I ever had in my life! It was many years after the war ended before I got this story collaborated, most people I told just thought I had been dreaming!.

As can be imagined diarrhoea was rife, and the sight of men squatting in all sorts of places became commonplace, even on one occasion in the middle of the main street of a small town, much to the astonishment of a local inhabitant. One of the most bizarre sights were the war memorials to the dead of World War I in nearly every town and village through which we passed. It was almost like walking through towns and villages in England, and proved conclusively the utter futility of war, if we did not already know it. The details of this forced march are in a letter written to the Swiss Commission acting as protecting powers, signed by the camp Medical Officer, and our own camp leader Peter Thomson, an Australian. For the record this is printed in full in the Appendices to this book, and although accurate, it does in no way explain the terrible hardship we endured on that march, particularly at night in temperatures well below –10 degrees centigrade, with snow turning our ears, nose, eyes and all other parts of our faces into frosted accoutrements, and most of us wearing clothing completely unsuitable for those arctic conditions.

The final train ride with 55 or more people in a horse truck was an unbelievable experience, and unless one was a participant, very hard to understand the cruelty of a nation who allowed men to be cooped up in a truck for 4 days with virtually no food, little water, no sanitation whatsoever, and access to the outside world limited to an absolute minimum. It was no wonder that when arriving in the camp at Luckenwalde those involved were in most cases in a pitiful condition. Escape was virtually impossible and the German threat of death for any person falling out on the march never materialised, which was as well, as on our arrival there were a considerable number missing, mostly through sickness. Our 'Man of Confidence' (our liaison with the Germans who spoke the language fluently) Ron Meade, dropped out of the march with foot trouble, was released by the Russians and arrived back in the UK in March 1945. He lived in Luton and after I arrived home, learnt from my parents that he had visited them and updated them as to my condition when he had last seen me.

Luft 3a, Luckenwalde

Our trek from the railway station in the town of Luckenwalde was a miserable procession, and needs no imagination, but at least on our arrival at the camp some preparation had been made, and after the by now typical German efficiency in admitting us, we were ushered into the compound, and straight into the shower room. None of us, without exception had removed our clothes for the previous three weeks, and the bliss of the hot water, yes hot water was an incredible delight. During our march cigarettes had been very few, and usually shared between some 40 persons (one puff each) but now we were given two all to ourselves (lung cancer was far removed from our thoughts in those days.)

This was a very cosmopolitan camp with prisoners of many nationalities, and from all services, and our own compound was next to the Americans. The German guards were all of an age group, with the exception of Officers and NCOs in the region of 55 to 65, and most galling of all, armed with British Lee Enfield rifles. Rations issued on a daily basis, and we were assured by the guards the same as theirs, consisted of half a cup of soup (if that is what it could be called) 3 or 4 very small potatoes and 1/10th loaf of ersatz black bread, subsequently reduced to 1/12th (to demonstrate, 1/12th equates to one thick slice)

Compared with the Russian prisoners who were in a compound quite close by, this was luxury, when one considers that these poor wretches were marched out of camp every day to work. They were in a very bad condition, both in health and dress, and yet we were virtually powerless to do anything to help them. There was also a large French contingent who did not endear themselves to very many of the other inhabitants, being virtually in charge of the rackets which prevailed (I should add almost all involving food) and seemed to be very co-operative with the Germans.

Life here for the first few weeks was black indeed, diarrhoea and even dysentery in extreme cases was rife, and the toilet block was the busiest of anywhere else in the camp. Long queues formed to see the Doctor, but he was powerless to help and could only advise us to toast the black bread into charcoal in an attempt to alleviate the sufferer. He was able to offer little sympathy, having virtually no medical supplies, as a potential patient in the sick row one day found to his cost. Everywhere there was filth and squalor, and with the lack of disinfectant for the kitchens and toilets, it was a miracle there was not a serious epidemic.

However with true British phlegm things gradually improved, due to some parcels both Red Cross and personal, being released, providing a slight variation in our food ration, plus a cache of cigarettes, intended for named POWs and sent by their relatives and friends, being distributed to all and sundry irrespective of the recipients name. At least this meant that we were able to maintain our "brews", something every ex POW will remember with joy, and although there was little or no fuel for the fires in the barracks the "blower" came into its own. This was an ingenious device which enabled one, by turning a handle furiously, to boil cans of water in an incredibly short time, using any scraps of fuel available. The better the design and construction of the blower, the shorter the boiling time, and with some the volume of air produced by the fan in the chamber was quite incredible.

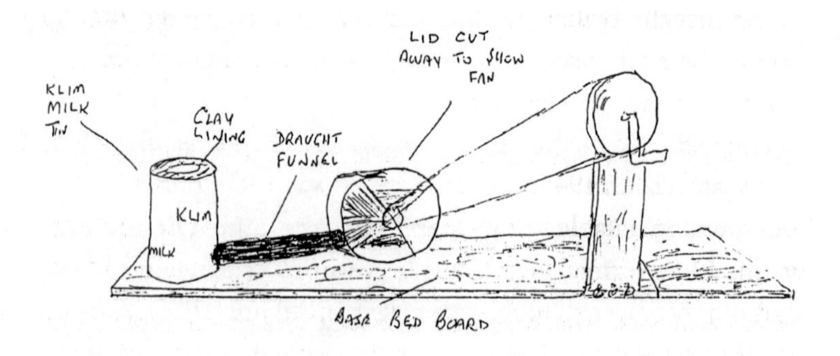

The news obtained from our illicit radio and given daily to each room in our block showed the improving war situation with the Russians still advancing from the East and the British, Canadians and Americans were poised on the edge of the Rhine. I had no idea how anyone managed to bring the radio from our previous camp, where it was kept or who listened to it, but as long as service was maintained, I was not much worried.

It was also during this period that Mosquito bombers of Bomber Command made their regular visits to Berlin – much to our delight. One evening in the hut, sometime approaching 'lights out', a German Officer in Parachute Regiment uniform entered and much to everyone's amazement it was Max Schmeling, a previous holder of the World Heavyweight Boxing title. From the reception he received, no one would have believed he was an enemy. He stayed for some considerable time happily answering questions and signing autographs!

As Spring began, with the news of the Allied forces crossing the Rhine, spirits in the camp rose, and with the approach of the Russians from the East it became apparent that we were going to be the middle of the 'sandwich', positioned as we were, some 14 miles south west of Berlin, in direct line with both armies. Little did we know then that the politics of war would decree that the British, Canadian and American troops would stop at the Elbe, leaving the Russians to take Berlin. What a change in history there would have been if the Arnhem attack had been a success.

By late March 1945, it was obvious that the end of the Third Reich was inevitable – the question was simply when and by whom. Our German guards were very chastened, some already seeking ways and means of avoiding their impending imprisonment and all very uncertain of their future. We had instructions from our Senior British Officer, Wg/Cdr Beaumont (of Typhoon, Tempest and, after the war, Lightning fame) that no escapes should be attempted. Few of us had the strength to do this anyway! Although spirits remained high our physical condition did not improve, and if anything deteriorated, with our German rations unchanged but by now all Red Cross parcels exhausted.

The noise of battle could be heard getting closer and closer, and there were frequent air battles overhead, with German aircraft and what appeared to be obsolete Russian Fighters. The Royal Air Force and the 8th American Air Force were also very much in evidence, and we had a grandstand view. But those of us with Bomber Command experience lay with apprehension as stray aircraft went over at night, knowing that this was usually when they released hung up bombs.

A night raid on Potsdam in early April was an incredible experience, and the noise and light in the sky made it almost unnecessary to use a light to read.

In the second week of April there occurred a most surprising event, when a number of RAF prisoners, including me, were told to gather their gear together, such as it was, and prepare to be transferred to Munich on the Fuhrer's orders to be held as hostages. We marched – or should I say straggled – to the railway station in Luckenwalde, and in a siding adjoining the main platform, were several of the now familiar trucks (6 horses/40 men), where we were placed aboard some 50 per truck. Each truck was allocated a Guard, and ours became most friendly, and told us he had served in the first war, he was now nearly 65 years of age, had been a Guard on a train, who arriving at his home station one evening a few months previously was told he was now in the army. He had a Lee Enfield rifle as explained earlier, and while he was showing us photographs of his wife and children, we removed the magazine, took out the bullets, and placed them in his overcoat pocket. This prank did not make us too popular with our senior officers, as we had forgotten in our youthful exuberance that this could have led to an unwanted search!

We were terrified at the thought of travelling by train so close to the battlefront, as we were well aware of the devastation being caused to trains by Allied rocket-firing aircraft. As a precaution we painted P-O-W in large letters on the roof of the trucks (with the exception of one marked G-O-O-N-S!).

One incident remains, during a period when we were allowed off the train, when a typical young SS Officer tried to impose his authority on a crowd of youngsters who had come to stare at the strange looking men standing in the siding. The boos and jeers which emanated from the ranks of the POWs soon made him aware that he was fighting a losing battle, and he disappeared from the scene.

Fortunately, no engine arrived to tow our trucks and on the 14th April we returned to camp. The day before we left the station we heard of the death of the American President, Franklin D. Roosevelt – but of course we could not reveal to our guards that we knew.

Our arrival back in camp caused some consternation, firstly because we were not expected back, and secondly because all the space we had previously occupied had been reallocated. Also, when leaving the compound on the way to the station we had each been relieved of one of the two blankets in our possession, but these was not returned to us, leaving us colder than ever on the still wintry nights.

Somehow, things were sorted out, and we were re-housed, but then began what was probably the most traumatic experience of my life.

The war was catching up with us rapidly, and we found ourselves at the centre of a mortar battle between the advancing Russians and the embattled remains of a crack SS division who had visited our camp only the day before. On two occasions, German aircraft strafed the camp in the middle of the night, but fortunately without any casualties among the inmates. However, the psychological effect on us was another matter... the queues for the toilets were greater than ever, and not because of the food! It was certainly a period for keeping 'your head below the parapet' when outside the hut, although it is astonishing what a false sense of security a wooden building can give you!

| CHAPTER 9 |

Release & Repatriation

Friday the 20th April was the day when we woke to find that we were masters of our own destiny. The German guards had all left the camp, with the exception of some half dozen, and these had surrendered themselves to us, and had thrown their weapons into the lake alongside the camp. The administration building had been left completely intact, and all documents were returned to the individual prisoners, giving a complete record of their captivity. Saturday was almost an anticlimax, nothing much happened or changed, and we went to bed with all the rumours of release ringing in our ears. On Sunday morning (22nd April) we awoke to the roar of Russian tanks, who had entered the camp, and were occupied in knocking down all the barbed wire – much to the annoyance of those in responsible positions, who preferred the wire to remain to segregate the various factions in the compounds.

Order was at last restored, the tanks proceeded to the compound where the Russian prisoners were housed, and those capable of holding a gun were installed on a tank, and all then left the camp, and we did not see them again.

We were free! Or were we? From the very first it was obvious that the Russians who eventually arrived to take over the camp had other ideas. We were told that we must be patient, nobody must leave the camp, but to wait transport when available. Two members of the RAF contingent had already lost their lives trying to break out over the wire just prior to our release, which was a clear sign to most of us that patience was essential.

Some 7-10 days after our release a sad and sombre ceremony was organised by our Russian liberators, when a parade was held complete with Newsreel cameras, and the remaining Russian prisoners, mostly very sick, and in many cases unable to walk, were taken from the camp with much pomp and ceremony. We could only hope that they were received as warmly and sincerely in their homeland.

Our immediate priority had to be the feeding of those prisoners in the RAF compound, and to this end the Russians provided armed guards to protect our own scavenging parties, who went into the surrounding countryside to round up cattle for butchering to provide food. The advancing Russian army was not geared to supply any but their own troops, and largely lived off the land as they advanced. In the interests of self-preservation we rapidly became self-sufficient, but food was still very scarce, and certainly not adequate for normal needs. Adding to the problems within the camp was the influx of refugees in their thousands, all of whom had fled in the face of the Russian advance.

Life became a day to day existence in more ways than one, with rumour and counter rumour paramount. I personally joined the wiring party who repaired all the telephone lines so that communication could be resumed.

A daily news bulletin was started, using the existing facilities in the administration block, giving information on the local state of affairs, particularly with reference to refugees and military personnel, plus most importantly of all, the war situation and how it could affect us. Copies of these daily bulletins, including the King's speech can be found in the Appendices.

The situation did not improve. By this time there were 16,000 mixed nationalities within the camp, and because of this deterioration, by letter to the Russian authorities on the 7th May the Senior British Officer gave notice that from then on he would only be responsible for the British. This letter is reprinted in its entirety in the Appendices to this book, and will give and indication of the situation which prevailed at that time.

VE day came and went, but still nothing happened. As can be seen from the letter, a contingent of Americans arrived and we were told that trucks would arrive the next day, as the first stage of our repatriation. The trucks arrived the next day as promised, but the Russians would not allow anybody to embark, using their rifles to reinforce their instructions, and the trucks went away again, empty!

A few of the more headstrong decided to be masters of their own destiny, and left the camp to walk West in the hope of meeting up with British forces. My old colleague Frank was among them, and meeting up with him much later it turned out that despite difficulties, they had been successful and arrived back in the UK much earlier than the rest of us.

The next two to three weeks are but vague memories. The Russian authorities did their best to improve our situation, which included a move to the barracks previously occupied by the German guards and, although they bore a heavy smell of garlic or something similar, they were much more comfortable than the huts. Food was still scarce although we were no longer starving, but children from the local town, begging for food for themselves and their families, now constantly pestered us. The roles were now reversed. Some of the more intrepid kregies made trips into the town of Luckenwalde, but this was not advisable in view of the activities of the Russian troops roaming the town and its surrounds.

At last we were told to pack our belongings (which was not very difficult, as by this time we had virtually only what we were wearing) because the trucks would be arriving tomorrow… And they did! American trucks, but with Russian drivers. Registration, previously a cause for delay, was completely dispensed with, and after only a few minutes we all climbed aboard.

The Russian drivers had no convoy discipline whatsoever, and each in his own way and in his own time, made his way through the woods south of Berlin, where there was still much evidence of the ravages of war, and even some charred bodies still hanging in the trees. No bridges had been repaired and no roads made up. Where there was damage the area had to be skirted, as in some cases bridges were completely down. Eventually we reached the banks of the river Elbe, and as we walked across the wooden pontoon bridge in one direction, Russian ex-prisoners were doing the same the opposite way. Waiting for us on the other side were a fleet of American trucks with drivers, but this time we left in orderly convoy, and it was very noticeable that all bridges had been repaired and all roads made up, making a very smooth ride indeed. The difference was quite startling, but much more important it was more comfortable. Our destination was the American base at Halle Leipzig, which we reached in late afternoon.

By this time it should be remembered, that with few exceptions, we were still wearing the clothes we were in when shot down and captured with very few opportunities during the past six months to clean them. This became a matter for concern when it was realised that we had female company once again (can you imagine a US base without it?), and repairs were immediately called for to rectify the neglect of the last traumatic few months. I have never seen clothes, particularly trousers, so quickly repaired in all my life! Such was the impact of a few ladies! In hindsight I recall that those we met in the Russian army did not have the same effect. In fact it was difficult to recognise them as women under their uniforms. One other observation that has remained with me was the whiteness of the bread we were given with our first meal. It was even whiter than that being issued before we left the UK on our last trip, and infinitely better both in looks and taste than the German black bread, we had endured for the last few months. With typical American generosity we were given all assistance possible in respect of food and drink (non-alcoholic) but for obvious reasons they were unable to assist with clothing, as our stay was very brief this was of no consequence.

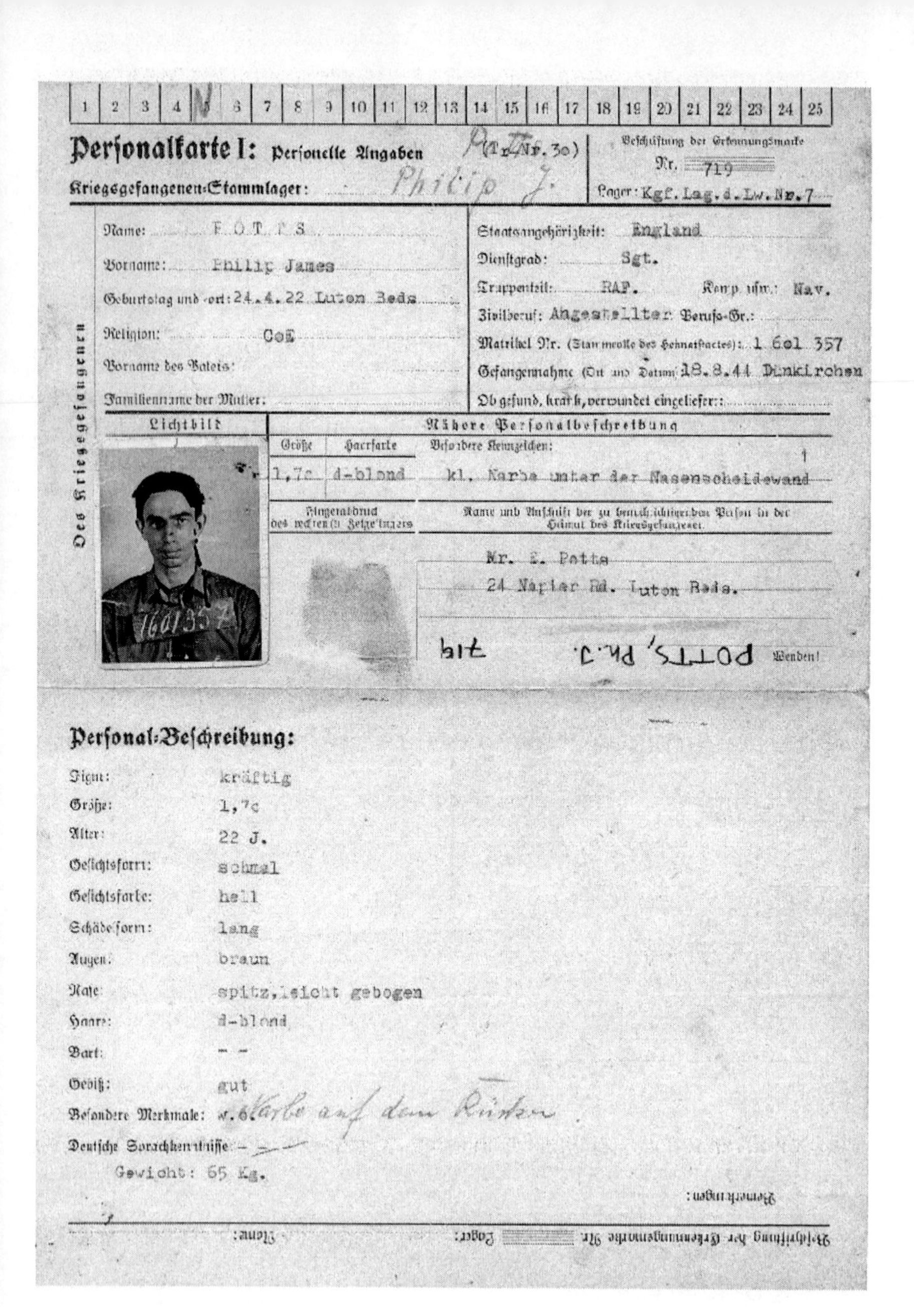

Personalkarte I: Personelle Angaben (Kr.-Nr. 30)
Kriegsgefangenen-Stammlager: Philip J.

Beschriftung der Erkennungsmarke Nr. 719
Lager: Kgf. Lag. d. Lw. Nr. 7

Des Kriegsgefangenen

Name: P O T T S
Vorname: Philip James
Geburtstag und -ort: 24.4.22 Luton Beds
Religion: CoE
Vorname des Vaters:
Familienname der Mutter:

Staatsangehörigkeit: England
Dienstgrad: Sgt.
Truppenteil: RAF. Komp. usw.: Nav.
Zivilberuf: Angestellter Berufs-Gr.:
Matrikel Nr. (Stammrolle des Heimatstaates): 1 601 357
Gefangennahme (Ort und Datum): 18.8.44 Dünkirchen
Ob gesund, krank, verwundet eingeliefert:

Lichtbild

1601357

Nähere Personalbeschreibung

Größe	Haarfarbe	Besondere Kennzeichen:
1,70	d-blond	kl. Narbe unter der Nasenscheidewand

Fingerabdruck des rechten (!) Zeigefingers

Name und Anschrift der zu benachrichtigenden Person in der Heimat des Kriegsgefangenen:
Mr. E. Potts
24 Napier Rd. Luton Beds.

719 POTTS, Ph. J.

Wenden!

Personal-Beschreibung:

Figur: kräftig
Größe: 1,70
Alter: 22 J.
Gesichtsform: schmal
Gesichtsfarbe: hell
Schädelform: lang
Augen: braun
Nase: spitz, leicht gebogen
Haare: d-blond
Bart: – –
Gebiß: gut
Besondere Merkmale: w. 6. Narbe auf dem Rücken
Deutsche Sprachkenntnisse: – –
Gewicht: 65 Kg.

Bemerkungen:

Beschriftung der Erkennungsmarke Nr. Lager: Name:

The Author's POW record card, rescued from the Admin block of Stalag Luft 3a.

| CHAPTER 10 |

Home at Last!

We were flown out, in a trusty Dakota after only two days, our next destination being Brussels, where we understood there was a large transit camp arranging final repatriation. This was organised by the Canadians, and a copy of the briefing sheet and camp lay-out can be found in the Appendices.

A fascinating experience awaited us. No doubt, as we were probably some of the last POWs to be evacuated they had learned how to cope, but it was still a lesson in administration and organisation of the highest order, and a credit to the Canadians in charge.

You entered one end of the system as a dirty, scruffy, unkempt individual, and arrived at the end having been cleaned, identified, documented, deloused, kitted-out with clean new clothes, washing and toilet facilities, cigarettes and money. My only complaint was that I was now in an army uniform, which was all that was available, but it was a small price to pay for being clean and tidy once again. We were given the freedom of the camp and the town, with only one instruction, "be here at 8 o'clock in the morning or you may miss your flight home".

We did not need to be told this twice! Facilities in the camp for food, cinema and entertainment were open all night, and as one would imagine sleep was the least of our worries, although we had all been provided with a bed. We had been provided with a little local currency and three or four of us did venture to the bar in town located nearest to the camp, and it was here I had my first experience of mixed toilets when an elderly lady opened the door. This must have caused some shock to our systems, which were still at a low ebb, and we did not outstay our welcome.

We were fortunate that our flight was called the very next morning. We discovered that we were to be flown home, as we had arrived – by a fleet of Lancaster bombers, and they were a joy to behold when we arrived at the airfield. We left eventually just about lunch time, and as I was positioned behind the Navigator's table, felt very much at home and had a good view of our course home, which was virtually a reversal of our ill-fated trip months before. Bomb craters near the old flying bomb sites could still be seen and I wondered if any of them were ours. The White Cliffs of Dover eventually came into view, a sight to remember, and shortly afterwards in the early afternoon we landed at an aerodrome in Southern England. HOME AT LAST!

The Royal Air Force did their best to make us welcome, but at the time it seemed they were not prepared for us, perhaps being Saturday and we were so far behind everyone else we were not expected. However tea and refreshments were prepared and served and later the same day we were coached to a station (I know not where) and sent on our way by train to Cosford.

It was here that the organisation of the Royal Air Force really came into its own. It was nearly midnight when we arrived, but the reception was absolutely superb, and virtually faultless in its simplicity even though this was Saturday night 27th May 1945, almost exactly six weeks since we had been released by the Russian army. Having identified ourselves, been given a cable form to advise our families that we were home, we were shown to our sleeping quarters, where all beds had been made up and "joy of joys" clean sheets and bedding at last!

Sunday was spent in rekitting ourselves, with an army of WAAFs on hand to sew BREVETS, STRIPES etc. on uniforms, which tailors had ensured fitted properly. Other formalities were completed during the day, which included a debriefing about our last trip, and providing any information relative to our capture and captivity. By the end of the afternoon we were ready to leave, but only those who lived close to Wolverhampton were allowed, and the rest of us had to spend one more night.

With leave passes for eight weeks and ration cards containing double rations, on Monday morning we were at last on our way to London, and thence to Luton, arriving at approximately 4 o'clock that afternoon. Only one taxi was available, and I was asked by a civilian if he could take it before me as he was in a hurry. After the traumas of the previous few months it seemed churlish to refuse. After all, what was a few more minutes at a time like this. I returned home at last, to be greeted on the doorstep by my young niece of 4, who did not recognise me, and then to see my mother who I had not expected to see again.

IT WAS GOOD TO BE HOME!

The Aftermath

The first few days at home were spent in renewing acquaintanceship with family and friends, and much to my surprise on one occasion a friend of long standing hailed me in the street with the comment "I though you were dead!" This made me realise just how lucky I had been. I had returned, and as far as I knew, completely unharmed, although some three stone lighter in weight.

But all the traumas were not completely over. I still had to meet my skipper Johnnie's parents and cousin, and their distress was probably not helped by seeing me alive. When we eventually met it was very sad indeed. I realised that the distance between death and life was so slight – in my case the proximity between Ken, Johnny and myself was only a few feet. They were dead and I still living.

During my stay in Germany I had received no correspondence at all and although my parents had received some they knew I was a Prisoner of War when advised in October that my name was revealed in a Lord Haw Haw broadcast. Later they were also advised of this by the Air Ministry and the Royal Air Force Benevolent Fund.

The eight weeks leave originally granted was extended by two weeks, and after returning to Cosford for medicals, briefing and consultations which only lasted a few days, I was sent on indefinite leave which eventually extended to a further eight weeks, and was probably the reason I lost contact with Jim Davies for so many years.

It was during this period that the war in the Far East ended with the dropping of the atom bombs on Japan, but this time I was in my own home town to savour in full the celebrations of VJ day. In fact a small party of us on leave at the time celebrated from the time the first bomb was dropped, until several days after the war had actually finished!

Most of the rest of my time in the service was rather an anticlimax. I was called back from leave after the eight weeks stated above, reporting to RAF Wittering for more consultations and assessments, and in fact was requested to return to flying duties, which would have meant "signing on" until the end of 1947. But at this stage I did not consider this an acceptable suggestion, and rather agreed to retrain until such time as I would be demobilised.

Again sent on indefinite leave, I eventually after five weeks received a posting to Cheddington, quite close to Luton, but on arrival nobody knew what I was supposed to do. Fortunately after a discussion with the CO, I was requested to join the team in the Equipment Branch, which appealed to me, in view of my potential return to civilian life and was something quite closely akin to my occupation before enlisting in the Royal Air Force.

A few tranquil weeks ensued as I learned the rudiments of the service stores system. Then, due to the good offices of the CO, I was posted to Group HQ at Langley and subsequently to Medmenham, just outside Marlow, a most pleasant part of England. I was to serve on the staff of the Equipment Officers who at that time were in the process of re-equipping and updating a number of the wartime aerodromes. This proved to be a most interesting and instructive period, and I became so involved that I began to have thoughts of applying to make this my future career. In true service style, however, the inevitable happened, I was suddenly posted, and despite the unsuccessful intervention of my CO, a Group Captain, I was on my way to Bassingbourn, Cambridgeshire, as an Air

Movements Officer. One can imagine the look of astonishment on the fact of the Adjutant, when my reply to his question of "where did you train" was "nowhere". This rather placed a completely new picture on my career, and after a discussion with the Adjutant, I found that I was entitled to leave the service, and decided that under the circumstances this was the correct decision.

And so I returned to civilian life!

Many times since I have been asked "Was it worth it?"

My answer is and always will be "YES!" The companionship and fellowship of those wartime RAF days would be impossible to find anywhere else, and as a young man I was proud to be doing my duty. Having said that, I must add, that my experiences also proved to me beyond doubt the complete and utter folly of war, and like many others who came very close to death on several occasions, I became convinced that a greater power is protecting and guiding us.

I rejoined Percival Aircraft in Luton in September 1946.

APPENDICES

For the attention of the Swiss Commission, acting as Protecting Power.

REPORT OF A FORCED MARCH MADE BY OCCUPANTS OF STALAG LUFT 7, GERMANY.

On January 17th, 1945, at approximately 11 am we received notice of one hour in which to pack our kit and be ready to leave the Camp by marching. At the same time we were informed by Ober Feldwebel Frank that for every one man who fell out of the column on the march, five men would be shot. This order was never given in writing.

The start was postponed until 3.30 am on January 19th. During the interval 68 sick men were evacuated to the civilian Ilag at Kreuzberg. We believe they were later taken to Stalag 344, at Lamsdorf.

Each man was issued with two-and-a-half days marching rations before leaving. When the march began at 3.30 am on January 19th, no transport was supplied for any sick who might have fallen out on the march and the only medical equipment carried was that carried by the Medical Officer and three Sanitators on their backs.

Details of march.

January 19th: Left Bankau and marched to Winterveldt, a distance of 28 Kms. This was done under extremely trying weather conditions and severe cold. The only accommodation at Winterveldt was small barns.

January 20th: Marched from Wintersveldt to Karlsruhe arriving at 10 am. We set off at 5 am and marched a distance of 12 kms. At Karlsruhe we were housed in an abandoned brick factory. Here for the first time we were provided with two field kitchens with which to cook for 1550 men. Each field kitchen was actually capable of cooking sufficient food for 200 men. The Medical Officer was also provided with a horse and cart for the transport of the sick. The cart was big enough to hold 6 sitting cases. Coffee was provided and after a rest period of 11 hours we were again ordered to move. The Camp Leader and the Medical Officer protested against further marching until the men were adequately fed and rested. We were told by the German Abwehr Officer that it was an order and must be complied with. The same night we left Karlsruhe and marched to Schönfeld, arriving at 9 am on January 21st, covering a distance of 42 kms. The conditions during the night were extreme, the temperature being -13 degrees Centigrade. The Medical Officers wagon was filled after the first five kilometres and from onwards, men were being picked up at the roadsides in a collapsed and frozen state and it was only by sheer will-power that they were able to finish the march. After crossing the river Oder, a distance of 34 kms., we were told that we would be accommodated and that no move would be made for two days.

January 21st. At Schönfeld we were accommodated in the cowsheds and barns of a farm. A room was provided for the sick at Lossen. Rations issued were about 100gms. of biscuits per man and half a cup of coffee.

January 22nd: At 3 am. orders were given by the Germans to prepare to march off at once. It was dark and there was some delay in getting the men out from their sleeping quarters because they could not find their baggage. The German guards thereupon marched into the quarters and discharged their firearms. The column was marching again by 5 am: Twenty-three men, it was ascertained at this stage, were lost and their whereabouts are unknown. They may have been left behind asleep, or they may have escaped. Also, thirty-one men were evacuated(we believe) to Lamsdorf, but nothing further has been heard of them. We marched to Jenkwitz, a distance of 34 kms. and were housed at a farm in barns. Here we were issued with a total of 114 kgs. of . fat, 46 tins of meat, barley, peas, and threequarters of a pig. Soup was issued, the ration being about a quarter of a litre per man. No bread was issued.

January 23rd. Left Jenkwitz at 6 am and marched 20 kms. to Wanzen.

January 24th. We were rested the day at Wanzen, sleeping in barns. The revier was in a cowshed. 31 sick were evacuated to Sagan. 400 loaves of bread were issued.

January 25th. Left Wanzen at 4 am for Keidersdorf. Covered 30 kms.

January 26th. Spent the day at Keidersdorf. Issued with 600 loaves of bread to last for two days.
January 27th. Left Keidersdorf and marched 19 kms. to Pfaffendorff, where we arrived at night.
January 28th. Left Pfaffendorf for Standorf at 5 am and marched a distance of 21 kms. Issued with 24 cartons of knackerbrot, 150 kgs. margerine and 50 kgs. sugar. 22 sick were evacuated to Scheidnitz and eventually arrived at Sagan.
January 29th. Left Standorf at 6 pm and marched to Peterwitz a distance of 22kms. We arrived at 4 am the follwing day. This march was carried out in darkness under extreme conditions, with a blizzard blowing the whole time. The men arrived at Peterwitz in an utterly exhausted condition. Before leaving Stansdorf we were promised that we have to march no further as transportwould be supplied from Peterwitz. 104 kgs. of meat were issued, 1 sack of salt, 25 kgs. of coffee and 100 kgs. of barley.
January 30th. At Peterwitz 30 men from Stalag 344, who had been left without guards, joined our column. 296 loaves of bread were issued, 50 kgs. oats, and 35.5 kgs. of margarine
January 31st. We spent the day at Peterwitz. We were told that we would have to march to Goldberg before we got transport. 300 kgs. of oats were issued, 50 kgs. of coffee and 40 kgs. of margarine.
February 1st. We marched from Peterwitz to Prausnitz, a distance of 12 kms. We remained at Prausnitz from February 1st - 5th. On February 1st we were issued with 680 loaves of bread and 37.5 kgs. of margarine, 250
On February 3rd we were issued with 112.5 kgs. of margarine, 250 loaves, 100 kgs. sugar, 200 kgs. flour and 150 kgs barley. On February 4th the issue was 150 loaves. At night on February 4th the Commandant (Oberst Leutnant Behr) visited the farm and read out an order from OKW to the effect that five men were to be released and would be liberated at the first opportunity. The purpose of this we were unable to understand.
February 5th. Before leaving we were issued with 500 loaves of bread, 95 kgs. of margarine and 530 tins of meat. We were marched from Prausnitz to Goldberg, a distance of 8kms. On arrival at Goldberg we were put into cattle trucks, an average of 55 men to each truck. By this time there were numerous cases of dysentry and facilities for men to attend to personal hygiene were inadequate. The majority had no water on the train journey for two days. When the men were allowed out of the trucks to relieve themselves, numerous of the guards ordered them back inside again and we had to be continually getting permission for the men to be allowed out. We were on the train from the morning of February 5th until the morning of February 8th. Before commencing this journey, we were issued with sufficient rations for two days. The total distance marched was 240 kms:
SUMMARY.
As a result of this march and the deplorable conditions, the morale of the men is extremely low. They are suffering from an extreme degree of malnutrition, and at present, an outbreak of dysentry. There are numerous cases of frost bite and other minor ailments. They are quite unfit fot any further movement. Food and better conditions are urgently required. We left Bankau with no Red Cross supplies and throughout the march all the rations were short issued, the most outstanding being bread, which amounts to 2,924 loaves.

....
D. C. Howatson, R.A.M.C.,
Camp Medical Officer.

February 15th, 1945.

....
Peter A. Thomson, Pilot Officer,
R.A.A.F.,
Camp Leader.

The Royal Air Force Benevolent Fund.

PATRON: H.M. THE KING.
PRESIDENT: H.R.H. THE DUCHESS OF KENT.
CHAIRMAN: THE RT. HON. LORD RIVERDALE, G.B.E.

Telephone No.: HOVE 3992

All Communications to be addressed to the Secretary.

EATON HOUSE,
14, EATON ROAD,
HOVE, SUSSEX.

Our Reference SF V 5788 AMS 231.
Your Reference

12th March, 1945.

E. Potts Esq.,
24, Napier Road,
Luton,
BEDS.

Dear Sir,

I have to acknowledge with very sincere thanks, the receipt by this mornings post of your letter of the 8th instant, enclosing a Postal Order for 5/- as a donation to this Fund.

In enclosing our official receipt No. V. 5788, I am asked to convey the warmest thanks and very sincere appreciation ofLord Riverdale our Chairman and Members of Council, not only of the help so kindly and generously given in this material way, but in the sympathy and understanding shown in the future welfare of our gallant airmen and their dependants.

My Council share with you the good news that your son Sergeant P. J. Potts is safe, albeit a Prisoner of War in enemy hands and look forward to his safe return in the near future.

With renewed thanks.

Yours truly,

J. T. Carmichael.

Group Captain.
Deputy Secretary.

125 Ashton Rd
Luton
21/8/44

Dear Mrs Potts,

When I heard the news about Philip I hardly knew what to say to Mr Potts but I am sure he understood how what I really meant.

It's just as difficult to tell you, dear Mrs Potts, how much you are in the thoughts of many people during this time of deep anxiety. But so many of our dear lads have been found again even after sometime that there is still hope that his life has been spared.

May God help you to be brave to endure the suspense like so many other English mothers.

Yours very sincerely
Stanley J Bennett

Stanley Bennett was Organist/Choir Master at Christ Church where my father sang in the Choir.

LOCAL NEWS, 1530 HOURS, MAY 2nd, 1945

The situation concerning ourselves and the Stalin Camp is officially stated to be obscure. The Senior Allied Officer is still occupied with the matter and will make a statement about it immediately he is in a position to do so.

LOCAL MILITARY SITUATION

A little item of world news from the B.B.C. today was our local news. The B.B.C. Home Service News said this afternoon, "The survivors of German forces south-east of Berlin have been split into two and are being pounded to pieces by tanks and artillery in wooded country south of the Capital." According to latest reports from Luckenwalde, the pounding has ceased for today in any case and after yesterday's fighting at least a thousand German prisoners were seen being brought in. They were described by an Allied ex-prisoner as being in a worse condition physically than any prisoners he had ever seen. They were so tired and starved from their hiding in the woods that they could hardly drag their feet along. Many of them were wounded. The town today is quiet, much less Russian transport is passing through it and the machine gun posts which were put up last night have been removed. In part of the outskirts of the town yesterday evening there was some street fighting only a few hundred yards away from our own police headquarters. The prisoners who were seen being brought in were a very mixed lot and included S.S., ordinary garrison troops and Luftwaffe aircrew. Although the local military situation was well under control by last night, there was a great deal of noisy skirmishing within a few hundred yards of the wire in the woods east of the vorlager. At about dawn mortar shells were falling so close that one of our guardhouses was shaking with the explosions and a number of people greeted the dawn sitting in a cellar. The shells and machine gun bullets could be heard whistling through the wood as well as the shouts of the troops fighting there. A little while after dawn the fighting seemed to swing round to the south-east and south of the camp and later in the morning shells were crossing the Luckenwalde-Juterbog road.

One of our foraging parties today, on its way to Zulickendorf tried to reach the village through Frankenford, a little under five miles due east of Luckenwalde. There they found some of the front line reinforcements which had been sent for yesterday, dug in behind camoflaged machine gun and 40 mm. gun posts. The foraging party was halted by a very smart and friendly Russian officer who told them that it would be unwise to take the direct road to Zulickendorf as they might be fired on. The Russian officer said that Germans in this area had pretty well been broken up and invited the foraging party to have breakfast with him. When they proceeded on their way to Zulickendorf they encountered a large convoy of heavy tanks with 80 mm. guns and another convoy of 15 to 20 vehicles which looked like a staff headquarters moving west. The vehicles in this convoy had a very effective way of making civilian or non-operational vehicles pull to the side of the road and the first our foraging party knew about this was when some shots were fired into the air from an armoured vehicle coming up behind them. Some of these Russians said that they believed that American forces, according to their information, were only about 12 miles away to the west, and they hoped to join up with them at any time. The Russians are well established in Zulichendorf which is a few miles north-west of Frankenford. Three German prisoners were seen being brought in, two Luftwaffe and one army. They were escorted by a Russian with an unusual and impressive looking rifle and two-edged bayonet.

The following pages contain some pages of the daily newsletter produced at Stalag Luft 3a by the former Allied POWs after the surrender of the German guards.

This afternoon a column of German prisoners, totalling approximately 5,000 and spread over several miles along the road were seen going south from here on the main road to Juterbog. As far as could be seen, they were escorted by only two Russians, one at the front of the column and one at the end.

Foraging parties today brought in about six and a half tons of potatoes and twenty pigs, and they say that they have located twenty more for tomorrow. They have learnt their lesson for today in handling pigs and say that they have come back covered from head to foot in pig. One of the richest foraging areas for the camp is in the Zulickendorf area where the German Burgomaster is enthusiastically collaborating.

The German Commandant of the Adolf Hitler Lager is now struggling westwards somewhere through the woods hoping to make a successful and solitary crossing of the Elbe in search of the Americans. He was encountered by one of our out-of-camp workers in the woods a few days ago. He was an Oberst-Lieutenant, immaculately dressed in a civilian suit. Recent events seem to have made him rather cynical. He told the ex-prisoner of war who met him that on the previous day he had encountered three Hitler Jungend in the woods and they had asked him what he thought they ought to do. "I told them to go and find the Heldentod", said the Oberst as he trudged off through the woods trying to avoid it himself. The Russians were informed, but nothing further has been heard of this gallant officer.

Our police patrol from the town reports that the refugee situation in the past 48hours has been very bad. Refugees, mostly foreign workers and deportees, as well as prisoners of war, have been pouring through Luckenwalde, most of them with no idea of where to go, many without food and bare-footed. The food situation for the Germans in the town is not good. German civilians are allowed to buy 10 pfgs. worth of bread a day from the bakery which has been allotted to them. German money is still valid, but since the collapse no one has been paid any wages and there is not yet an organized food supply for the civilian population, which is already getting very hungry. There is absolutely no milk for any one at all to be found in the locality.

The Russians have been of great assistance to our Luckenwalde Police Patrol, now about 30 strong, in setting up a permanent headquarters, on the main road to Berlin, a few hundred yards from the Luckenwalde Town Hall. The Russians in the town yesterday invited some of the Allied Patrol to a celebration-of-May 1st breakfast. In yesterday's patrolling the Allied Police only took the names of about 60 prisoners of war from this camp who were on unauthorized visits to the town. This figure is considerably less than the previous day, but every one is warned that although our own Police Patrol goes off duty a little while before the 8 o'clock curfew comes into effect, the Russians enforce the curfew with great strictness and immediately place any unauthorized person under arrest.

Four Polish girls arrived in the camp today whose story is a first-hand testimony to the brutality and sadism of the Germans. In 1939 these girls--they were only 14 at the time--were sent to a forced labour ammunition factory at Radom in Poland. They worked there until 1944 when the approach of the Russians caused their removal into Germany. They were taken to a concentration camp where men and women were stripped naked in the street and examined by a German doctor. The fit were passed for work--the unfit for gas. These girls were employed in various factories working 12-hour shifts and were living in concentration camps. They were at Torgau when the approach of the

Americans caused the Germans to attempt to move them. They travelled 60 in cattle trucks which were locked and only opened once per day. They received one-tenth of a loaf per day and hardly any water. The trucks stood in Neu-Stettin railway yards sandwiched between an ammunition train and a petrol train. The siding was bombed and out of the 60 in one girl's truck, only she and four others escaped. They fled into the woods and eventually reached a foreign workers' camp where they were hidden until the Russians arrived. Conditions inside the concentration camps were described by these girls. They said that there were men and women S.S. guards and report that the women were worse than the men. The guards carried cat-of-nine-tails whichwere frequently used. Punishments consisted of stoppings of food, close confinement, kneeling down on gravel with their hands above their heads, and 25 lashes. They reported a case of a woman who broke a pane of glass while queuing up for food. The S.S. men in charge gave the whole barrack of 150 women 25 lashes each. These girls report as a matter of course that their heads were shaved and their identity numbers tattooed on their forearms. All four had been flogged on various occasions. They report that in six years of captivity they have received decent treatment from one German--a civilian foreman in a factory. None of these girls has any idea of the fate or whereabouts of their parents and families.

SUPPLY

As from tomorrow the Allied Supply Organization which has been feeding the camp will cater only for British, Americans, Norwegians, who total 10,000. The other nationalities, including some thousand Italians who have arrived in the past 48 hours, will come under the care of a specially appointed Russian Major.

The total of food which came into the Camp yesterday, May 1st, was: 172 sticks of sausage, 3,021 loaves of bread, 15 pigs, and three tons of potatoes.

Here are two camp appeals. Capt. Fareham, Guard Commander of the Vorlager gate, has in his possession a book called "Anatomy and Physiology". Contained in the book is quite an amount of personal mail belonging to Fusilier David McIntee, P.O.W. No. 26312. Capt. Fareham will return the book and mail upon application.

Lieut. Wilkinson, who is Officer in charge of women on the camp, says that he is a very harassed man. At present, and asks every one to stay away from his charges and not to pay them social calls.

AFTERNOON B.B.C. HEADLINES

7th Army forces have captured Field Marshal Von Runstedt, former C. in C. in the West.

British 2nd Army troops are 14 miles from Lubeck. The new German Fuehrer, Admiral Donitz, has appointed Count Steren Von Cosick, Foreign Minister in place of Ribbentrop who has disappeared. 5th and 8th Armies continue their advances in north Italy where prisoners now total 160,000. New Zealand forces have linked up with Marshal Tito's forces near Trieste. The German Commander in Chief in Norway says Hitler died a hero's death and the battle must go on. There is now direct telephone communication between Berlin and Moscow. A big battle is in progress in the Far East for Rangoon.

LOCAL NEWS, 1400 HOURS, MAY 5th, 1945

The Senior Allied Officer reports that the surgeon in charge of the convoy of 23 U.S. Army ambulances which arrived here at 1300 hours, Lieut. Col. D. W. Clotselter, of the 83rd Division, has given the following information.

The ambulance convoy will today evacuate the bulk of the American, British and Norwegian sick, and will return tomorrow for the balance.

A lorry convoy is on its way here, but the Lieut. Col. cannot give its time of arrival or strength because his division has been busy evacuating an ex-prison camp at Altengrabow. Altengrabow is in the Russian Occupation zone, but the prison camp there was liberated by the Americans. The bulk of the lorries for our evacuation have to come today from Hildesheim, just south of Hannover, 135 miles from here. They are bringing K-rations which will be issued to Americans, British and Norwegians immediately on arrival.

The following are the details which Lieut. Col. Clotselter has given to the Senior Allied Officer regarding standard evacuation routine which the 83rd Division has been using for other Camps.

Sick will be taken to Schonebeck, eight miles south south-east of Magdeburg, where they will be delivered to a Collecting Centre. From there, after treatment, the less serious cases will be flown home from Hildesheim. Serious cases will probably be sent back to Base Hospitals.

The fit will be taken by lorry via the American bridgehead over the Elbe at Zerbst, opposite Barby; and direct to Hildesheim, a distance of about 240 miles in all. From Hildesheim British personnel are flown direct to England, and American to the Channel Coast to await early departure to the United States. It is presumed that Norwegian personnel will proceed to England.

The Senior Allied Officer states, "I hope it will be possible to arrange for all British, Americans and Norwegians here to be evacuated by this procedure. Naturally it cannot be regarded as finally settled and we must await the arrival of the trucks."

LOCAL NEWS, 1730 HOURS, MAY 5th, 1945

Captain Sincavich, U.S. Army, a P.O.W. contact officer from S.H.Q.A.E.F. arrived in the Camp at 1630 today. He brought two lorry loads of bread and two of K-rations, which have already been handed over to Supply.

Captain Sincavich has given the following information to the Senior Allied Officer:

The main convoy of trucks will not arrive until tomorrow when, Captain Sincavich hopes, sufficient will come to complete the evacuation. They will bring more K-rations with them. As regards the route of our evacuation he says that the trucks will go to Schonebeck, eight miles south south-east of Magdeburg in the first instance, where it is possible that personnel will be transferred to a train for Hildesheim. Alternately the trucks may go right through to Hildesheim. The routine at Hildesheim is that ex-P.O.W.s are de-loused, reclothed if necessary, and generally dusted off. They are then formed into groups of 26 and flown off in C-47's, the British straight to England, and the Americans to the Channel Coast. The average stay at Hildesheim has been 24 to 48 hours and is to some extent dependent on flying weather.

Captain Sincavich took away with him nominal rolls of British, Americans and Norwegians and requested documents and information regarding German war criminals, which will be given to him tomorrow when he returns, as he hopes to do.

The Senior British Officer is communicating the following in writing to the Russian authorities here today.

FROM: Senior British Officer, Stalag IIIA

TO: Russian Commandant for Repatriation, Stalag IIIA

May 7, 1945

In order to avoid misunderstanding, I am putting into writing the principle statements which I made at our conference last night.

The situation of the British at this camp is now as follows. From 22nd April, I, at the request of the Russian Authorities have been responsible for the administration and security of this entire camp of 16,000 mixed nationalities. The work of the camp during this time has been carried out mainly by British and American officers and men. It should, however, be appreciated that, owing to the Russian orders re confinement to camp, etc. we have had to continue to all intents and purposes as prisoners. That these orders were a military necessity is of course clear, but nevertheless the result has been a lowering of the spirit of all ranks. It is important to understand and make allowances for the mental attitude of prisoners of war who have been liberated but are still denied their freedom.

The food situation; up to yesterday, was precarious, and the daily ration, even though assisted by American supplies, is still grossly inadequate. It is realized that the Russian authorities overcame great difficulties in providing food at all under harassing circumstances; but it will also be agreed that the supply organization of this camp performed most of the work. Furthermore, the camp has become even more overcrowded owing to the influx of Italian regugees. The problems of sanitation are considerable, and the general health is threatened.

In spite of all this, the Russian orders were obeyed and control was maintained up to the 5th of May. On that day an American officer, representing Supreme Allied Headquarters, arrived with instructions to evacuate the Americans and British in that order. His credentials were not accepted by the Russian authorities here, who stated that they could not allow such an evacuation to proceed since they had no orders on the subject. An ambulance convoy, which also arrived on this day, was permitted to evacuate all American and a few British sick.

Yesterday the American representative from Supreme Allied Headquarters returned with a convoy to carry out his orders. Capt. Tchekarev acting as deputy for Capt. Medvedev, who was sick, refused to allow him to proceed with his duties. Later, when an attempt was made to proceed with the evacuation, armed force was used against American troops to prevent their leaving the camp.

No doubt this whole affair is due to a misunderstanding, but the situation created is extremely serious. In spite of continual assurances that we were to be repatriated with the least possible delay, we now see the Russians actively preventing such repatriation. It is impossible for me to explain or justify such action in the eyes of my officers and men. I warned Capt. Medvedev on 4th May that such a situation was likely to arise, and that, if it did, I could not be responsible for the consequences.

Last night I was informed, for the first time, that the chief obstacle to our repatriation was that the registration was not complete. I have repeatedly offered to undertake the whole task of registration; I could have completed it by now if my offer had been accepted. In any case, I cannot believe that the Russians intend that vital interests should be threatened for the sake of a mere formality.

As the Senior British Officer here I am responsible, above all else, for the welfare of my officers and men. This welfare is seriously endangered by the present situation. I therefore demand that the position may be clarified without delay, and that our repatriation may be proceeded with immediately. Failing this, I must ask to be enabled to communicate with my Government.

Finally I must point out that the present situation renders my position as Senior Allied Officer untenable. I therefore resign that position and from now must be regarded as responsible only for the British.

LOCAL NEWS, 1700 HOURS, MAY 9th, 1945

At the time of going to press it is still officially stated that no information is available on the function of the Russian transport which arrived this morning.

Broadcasting to all Allied prisoners of war today, Allied Supreme Headquarters issued this message from General Eisenhower.

"The war with Germany is over. The German armed forces have been defeated. You have all played your part in bringing the war to a successful conclusion and you shall share the victory, your victory, which together we have won. You will be returned to your homes with all possible speed and to ensure this you must follow these instructions:

The Camp Leader will take over command of your Camp for all purposes. The Germans will maintain all essential services for each Camp. The Camp Leader now in command will look after your welfare and maintain discipline. Within ten days British and American officers of the A.E.F. will arrive in your Camp. Every P.O.W. will remain in his respective Camp until the arrival of these contact officers. You must stay where you are! Any movement will upset plans for your evacuation. The Contact Officers will make sure that you are moved as quickly as possible but nothing can be done until they arrive. So again I say stay where you are--stay put."

By midday today 32 voluntary evacuees from this camp were back where they started from. The total British personnel in the Camp is now 2,092.

Wing Commander Ingle, Russian Liaison Officer, states that those who return to the fold and fail to register with the Russians immediately will seriously prejudice the chances of the remainder of the British personnel of being quickly and smoothly evacuated when the Russians give the order. Every one who returns should be swiftly directed to the Russian Registration Office and to Wing Commander Ingle's office in order that the Russian Registration lists and our own nominal roll shall check up.

Some of the Allied ex-P.O.W.'s who took off on their own ten days ago to try and reach the linkup area near Torgau tell the following story:

"When we reached Juterbog we found that we could not get on the direct Dresden road to Torgau as there was a German pocket in the way. So with the help of Russian transport we turned south-east and reached Muskau on the first day. All that was necessary to get rides on Russian lorries was to ask one of the Russian girl traffic controllers to stop a lorry going our way. Our identity was never seriously questioned. The statement that we were British was almost always immediately accepted and we were sometimes embraced enthusiastically and invited at once to a celebration feast. At Muskau we were billeted in a big hotel which was the local Russian officers' mess. There we met our first Russian Air Force officers, a major and two captains.

They were the most smartly dressed and polished Russian officers we have yet seen. They were all three fighter pilots, the major, with 73 air victories, and the captains with about 50 each.

THE KING'S SPEECH, MAY 8th, 1945 - "VE" DAY

Today we give thanks to almighty God....Speaking from our Empire whose capital city, war-battered but not for one moment daunted or dismayed, speaking from London I ask you to join with me in that act of thanksgiving. Germany, the enemy who drove all Europe into war, has been finally overcome. In the far-East we have yet to deal with the Japanese, a determined and relentless foe. To this we shall turn with the utmost resolve and with all our resources. But at this hour when the dreadful shadow of war has passed from our hearts and homes in these islands we must at least make one pause for thanksgiving, and then turn our efforts to the tasks all over the world which peace in Europe brings with it.

Let us remember those who will not come back, their constancy and courage in battle, their sacrifices and endurance in the face of the merciless enemy. Let us remember the men of all services and the women of all services who have laid down their lives. We have come to the end of our tribulations and they are not with us at the moment of our rejoicing. Then, let us salute in proud gratitude the great host of the living who have brought us to victory. I cannot praise them to the measure of each one's services, for in total war the efforts of all rise to the same noble height and all are devoted to the common purpose. Armed or unarmed, men or women, you have fought, striven and endured to your utmost. No one knows that better than I do, and as your king I thank with a full heart those who bore arms so valiantly on land, on sea, and in the air, and all civilians who are shouldering their many burdens and have carried them unflinchingly without complaint. With these memories in our minds let us think what it was that has upheld us through nearly six years of suffering and peril; the knowledge that everything was at stake, our freedom, our independence, our very existence as a people, but the knowledge also that, in defending ourselves, we were defending the liberties of the whole world; that our cause not of this nation only, not of this Empire and Commonwealth only, but of every land where freedom is cherished and law and liberty go hand in hand. In the darkest hours we knew that the enslaved and isolated peoples of the earth looked to us, their hopes were our hopes, their confidence confirmed our faith. We knew that if we failed, the last remaining barrier against world-wide tyranny would have fallen in ruins. But we did not fail. We kept faith with ourselves and with one another, we kept faith and unity with our great allies. That faith, that unity, have carried us to victory, through dangers which at times seemed overwhelming. So let us resolve to bring to the tasks which lie ahead the same high confidence of our mission. Much hard work awaits us, both in the restoration of our own country after the ravages of war and in helping to restore peace and sanity to a shattered world. This comes upon us at a time when we have all given of our best. For five long years and more, heart and brain, nerve and muscle, have been directed upon the overthrow of Nazi tyranny. Now we turn, fortified by success, to deal with our last remaining foe.

The Queen and I know the ordeals which

We got onto the subject of tactics, types and performances right away. They said that their best and latest fighter was the "Mik", with a top speed of about 310 miles an hour. They thought that the Airacobra compared very favourably with any fighter they possessed, but obviously considered we were line-shooting when we told them of some of the speeds of our own aircraft. The latest Spits they had flown were Mark V, which they liked very much, but they refused to believe that the latest marks could be any better, "You can't change an aircraft as much as that", they said, "It's always the same aircraft no matter what you do to it". These three officers had fought in the Spanish Campaign and were now flying Yaks.

War damage at Muskau seemed very slight. The following day we went on to Sagan where we were billeted in a luxurious mansion, former home of the director of a bank. It was being used as the headquarters of a French General who was nominally in charge of tens of thousands of Frenchmen collected in the town. So many British and American ex-P.O.W.'s eventually arrived atthe mansion that the French General was left with only one room as his accommodation.

An American officer from this camp who had landed by parachute in Goering's back garden a few weeks before the end of the war during a Flying Fortress raid on Berlin, handled our liaison with the Russian Town Commandant. The Commandant would see this officer at times when he would refuse to see the French General. These visits were necessitated by the fact that occasionally the Russians forgot to supply us, but each time they were reminded they would send in supplies ranging from cigarettes to cattle without delay.

One part of Sagan town has been totally devastated though most of it has been untouched by the fighting. German prisoners are arriving there at the rate of 20,000 a day, and when we left there were reported to be 143,000 of them in the Stalag Luft III camps. From the first day of our arrival at Sagan we were promised that on the next day we should be given transport to the Allied line. One party of officers who got tired of waiting two days ago set out for Torgau but nothing has been heard of them since. Yesterday we left Sagan at four in the afternoon with six lorries under the impression that we were going on to the American lines. We arrived back here at two a.m. this morning.

The Sagan Russian Commandant told us yesterday that two days previously General Eisenhower had visited Marshal Konief's Headquarters there and had been entertained at a banquet.

The Russian authorities at Sagan have visited the Stalag Luft cemetery and placed flowers and wreathes on the graves of the 50 North Camp officers. Following this they took photographs of the graves and sent the negatives straight back to Moscow.

Copies of the VE-Day speeches by King George VI and Mr. Churchill can still be obtained in the Vorlager news room.

WAR CRIMINALS

The list of War Criminals which was handed to the U.S. authorities when they were in the camp included the names of several German officers, well known to members of the camp. Bemann, Sturzkopf, Simm, and Rademacher are included among the most notorious. Two Germans responsible for the shooting of an American Air Corps officer in the centre camp at Sagan - Hauptmann Seifert and Feldwebel Althof - are also listed. A member of the Gestapo group responsible for the murder of the British officers at the same camp is named by Group Captain Kellett. Apart from the Germans known to us personally for their incorrect behaviour and ill treatment of Allied officers and men, there is a very comprehensive list of the principle Nazis of Luckenwalde; many of their names have been supplied by Sergeant Major Henderson, British Man of Confidence in Stalag IIIA. Their offences range from pilfering of the Red Cross store to actual brutality and manhandling of Allied P.O.W.'s.

Hauptmann Bemann is charged with the deliberate destruction and theft of clothing and food belonging to British officers; he is further indicted with being "continually insulting to British officers in his remarks and bearing."

Major Sturzkopf - "Bulk Issue" - is charged with continual lying and misrepresentation to the calculated detriment of the interests of British prisoners, moreover he encouraged his soldiers to be as vicious and ruthless as possible during searches and thus caused wanton looting and destruction of their property. He sentenced many prisoners to the cells without a shred of evidence against them and was known to be generally deceitful and vicious.

Hauptmann Rademacher incited his soldiers to strike British officers with their rifle butts, he displayed a violent and uncontrollable temper and drew and fired off his revolver on numerous occasions with the idea of intimidating the prisoners or provoking an incident. He lost no opportunity of humiliating and ill-treating British officers and took a fiendish delight in the destruction of their clothing under the guise of searching them.

Last but not least there is Hauptmann Simm, the hotel manager, who probably achieved a greater personal loathing among Allied prisoners than any other of his colleagues. Possessed of a mean and spiteful nature, he did everything possible to make us uncomfortable or to humiliate us. He incited the Camp Commandant to take spiteful action against the prisoners and lost no opportunity of insulting them himself.

A case outside our own experience is that of Lieut. Janke, charged with brutality to the Polish officers of this camp during their move here. This brave German is now the possessor of a set of Polish papers taken from a dead Pole and is no doubt congratulating himself on his cunning; he is for the moment spared the knowledge that he is being searched for under his alias as well as his proper name and that his ponderous subterfuges were transparent from the first.

Lastly there is Obergefreite Gisevius who is perhaps typical of the whole Nazi system. For this Corporal had more power in Stalag IIIA than the Commandant himself. A rabid Nazi, he was "the power behind the throne" and dictated his wishes and commands to his superiors whenever he chose to do so. He was responsible for keeping many prisoners in the cells for months at a stretch without a trial and doing his best to deprive them of their food. Many eccentricities of German conduct are explained by the presence of such men as this corporal in the ranks of the German Army.

The list prepared by the Intelligence department here is by no means a complete one but when the list for all prison camps is compiled, no notorious German will escape.

LOCAL NEWS, 1200 HOURS, MAY 11, 1945

The following is a statement by the Senior British Officer to all British personnel:

"General Famin arrived here last night and left again early this morning. I was with him from 11 o'clock until 2 a.m. this morning.

He appeared to take an extremely grave view of the recent unofficial evacuation from this camp, and required me to provide him then and there with a written report on it. He also obtained a written report from the Senior American Officer.

He told me that the American General Hodges had confirmed that no orders had been given on the American side to evacuate this camp, and added that if any further British left the camp I would be interned.

Of course a British officer does not need to take any notice of this type of threat, but at the same time I must tell you again that any further unauthorized evacuation, apart from making my position impossible, will undoubtedly delay our repatriation.

It appeared that the General had expressed strong disapproval of the manner in which his staff here had looked after us, particularly in the matter of food, and he informed me that Captain Medvedev would be court-martialled.

I told him that in my opinion Captain Medvedev had done his best with the almost non-existent resources at his disposal.

With regard to the date of our repatriation, the only information I received was that the Russian authorities were now awaiting word from the British and Americans that they were ready to receive this camp.

I repeat the order which I issued on May 8th:

No British personnel are to leave the camp bounds except on duty."

The Senior British Officer addresses the following to all British personnel:

"I think that there has been a good deal of misunderstanding in the Camp regarding General Eisenhower's message to ex POW's, in which he said that contact officers would arrive within ten days. It must be realized that this can only apply to camps in the area scheduled for occupation by British and American troops, Obviously General Eisenhower cannot give direct orders about camps in the Russian zone.

Actually, as you know, we were visited by American contact officers on the 5th and 7th of this month, but it turned out that they had no authority to act in this area.

The British and American representatives concerned, with the repatriation of this and other camps in the Russian zone are members of a commission sitting in the Berlin area. I cannot say whether or not they will visit us, but I should think so.

As far as I can find out, it is now simply a question of laying on the transport; this may be either Russian or Anglo-American. It is hopeless to attempt to prophesy how long this will take. I half expect to see trucks arrive any day, but it could still be a fortnight. We must try and see the matter in its right proportion and not exaggerate our own importance. After all the war finished only just over a week ago.

Hanging about is indeed a great trial for all ex-prisoners, but if we can maintain a fairly philosophical attitude, the time of waiting will be more tolerable and even quite interesting.

Remember that once upon a time we were able to be cheerful with the certainty of many months and even years of captivity ahead. The prospect of a further few days or even a fortnight, when you come to think of it, should not really dismay us."

THE NORWEGIAN CONTACT OFFICER

The Norwegian Contact Officer returned from Marshal Koniof's Headquarters, which are now in Dresden, this morning. While there he had an interview with General Famin at which he offered to undertake the repatriation of all the Norwegian officers. He was told that his offer would have to be referred to the respective governments but in the meanwhile it was unlikely that the Norwegian officers would be repatriated via Murmansk, but would probably go via the Baltic. He was told that he could go ahead collecting transport. Before he left here this morning for Hamburg, the S.B.O. gave him the strength of the British personnel at this camp together with a description of the camp's conditions, for handing to the British authorities at Hamburg.

The BBC announced this evening at 1830 that General Otto Ruge has been liberated by the Russians from a German concentration camp, and he is now in Moscow on his way to Oslo.

CAMP BOUNDS

As a result of complaints of watch stealing by Russian troops, the Russians from last night put on guards around the outskirts of the Camp. This unfortunately cut across the bounds authorized by the SBO, and today a temporary arrangement was made by which the three ponds could be used this afternoon. It is hoped that by tomorrow the original bounds will have been agreed upon by the Russians. An order on this point will be issued as soon as an agreement is reached. During yesterday's watch-lifting operations by wandering Russians outside the Camp guns were drawn once and one Russian, in a dispute with another, received a slight wound in the hand. On another occasion one member of the RAF was stopped and searched by three Russians. When he made it plain he was British the Russians handed him back four of his cigarettes and a gold ring which they had taken from someone else. But this cannot always be relied on.

MAIL

A store of mail has been located in Luckenwalde and is to be brought up here for sorting. It is not thought likely that much of it will be of interest to British personnel, but a report on it will be made as soon as possible.

PARCELS

There are now between 30 and 40 parcels, mostly Red Cross, in our own store. The milk from these parcels has already been given to nursing mothers among the refugees. Now with the agreement of the Senior American Officer, the rest of the food in the parcels will be distributed among sick women and nursing mothers of the Dutch and Belgian refugee camp, and also to nine Czech girls who arrived recently and are still suffering from their terrible experiences in a concentration camp.

All civilians under British protection are to live in barrack block Z 6. It is hoped soon to arrange an RAF dance in the West Camp.

BOOKS FOR F 2

An appeal is made for English books for the labour squad of the Supply Organization. The squad numbers 70, mostly glider pilots and Arnheim paratroops, with a sprinkling of RAF NCO's. This squad is at immediate readiness for unloading duties 24 hours a day and must remain within call of F 2. Time hangs heavily during the long standby, and the Labour Squad, which is doing an essential camp service, would appreciate any reading matter which can be spared. Please hand your books to F 2.

LOST

On May 3, when kit was returned from the Adolf Hitler Lager, a 160-page manuscript, sewn up in white cloth, was missed. The package was marked, "The Log, Lloyds Bank, Wisbeach, Cams., England." It is possible that the package was in a white RAF-type kit-bag which is also missing. If found, please return to the Orderly Room, East Camp.

LOCAL NEWS

MAY 18, 1945

CONCENTRATION CAMP SURVIVORS AT STALAG IIIA

NAME 30 GERMAN WAR CRIMINALS

MURDER CAMPS

AT ORANIENBURG, GOLLNOW & FURSTENBERG

RIVAL DACHAU & BELSEN

THE BRITISH INTERROGATION CENTRE IN THIS CAMP IN THE PAST FEW DAYS HAS ENCOUNTERED FIRST HAND EVIDENCE OF GERMAN ATROCITIES COMMITTED AGAINST CZECH MEN AND WOMEN IN GERMAN CONCENTRATION CAMPS AND PRISONS. THE CZECHS WHO HAVE ARRIVED IN THIS CAMP HAVE BEEN ABLE TO GIVE THE NAMES OF AT LEAST 30 GERMANS, 8 OF THEM WOMEN WARDERS, WHO IN THE PAST FIVE YEARS HAVE BEEN GUILTY OF BARBAROUS AND INHUMAN TREATMENT. THE NAMES OF THESE GERMANS AND A FULL REPORT OF THEIR CRIMES IS TO BE FORWARDED TO THE ALLIED WAR CRIMES COMMISSION.

The story told by Mrs. Marie Seidlova, a 53-year old Czech woman of Terezin, reveals that Ravensbruck, which was almost entirely a women's concentration camp, was run as a murder camp for the disposal of old and unfit people, who were gassed and burned at the rate of over 7,000 a year. Two of the other Czech ex-prisoners are able to add to the list of sadistic torture tricks which the Germans are known to have used to make prisoners confess to the crimes with which they were charged.

FIVE YEARS OF TORTURE

Vaclav Jech of Borkovice, was arrested in November, 1940, on a charge of listening to the English wireless.

He was taken to the jail at Budejovice where he remained in an underground cell for six weeks for Gestapo "interrogation". During one of these visits by the Gestapo, he was stripped naked in a temperature of 26 degrees below zero Centigrade, and in addition to being kicked and beaten with rubber truncheons, jets of ice cold water from a hose pipe were directed into his eyes and ears until he fainted. He was released after signing a document undertaking not to work against the Third Reich in thought or deed. The penalty for disobedience was shooting by the Gestapo. In June, 1941, Jech was arrested again after the Germans had found him working for the Czech National Resistance Committee. He remained in Budejovice prison until January, 1942, at intervals being beaten up, and once stabbed in the back with an officer's sword.

ORANIENBURG CONCENTRATION CAMP

In January, 1942, Jech went to one of the first concentration camps established by Hitler at Oranienburg just north of Berlin. Here among a party of 450 others he was put into a working party making bricks. Morning appel was at 5.00 a.m. and lasted an hour. Evening appel started at 6.00 p.m. and lasted two or three hours, according to the time the German officer in charge cared to delay his appearance. There were regular beatings-up in the brick works every day, and Jech estimates that the S.S. guards beat four or five persons to death daily.

On one occasion a Russian was seen by an S.S. guard to pick up a carrot that had fallen from a cart. After evening appel he was kept on the parade ground, and although there was a heavy frost and snow on the ground he was stripped and made to hold the carrot with both hands at arms-length. After an hour he fainted and the process was repeated when he revived. Whenever his arms began to sink, cold water was poured over his face to stop him from fainting. After three hours of this, other prisoners were allowed to carry him into the barracks where he died five hours later.

In June, 1944, Jech was taken for interrogation to the Gestapo prison at Terezin. In July a number of Czech officers, among them a general, was taken to this camp from Pilsen. Jech himself witnessed the general with his hands tied to his ankles kicked across a court yard for 300 yards. His mouth had been filled with salt, and he was gagged with a scarf. On another occasion the Germans ordered a Jew in the camp to hang himself by morning, adding that if he failed to do so, five others would die. The Jew carried out his own execution. In August, 1944, Jech was at an S.S. camp in Brandenburg. During an air raid the camp kitchen was hit and some of the Russian prisoners picked up scattered pieces of bread. The German camp commandant shot five of them dead with a rifle. Their bodies were left lying where they fell for a week.

INTERROGATION BY BARBED-WIRE BEATING

Another member of the Terezin Gestapo prison was Jaroslav Karban, a former police inspector, who was arrested in June, 1944, of helping the Czech patriot organization. Out of a total of 80 others who were interrogated with him, only two were released, the remainder were beaten with rubber truncheons packed with barbed-wire until they confessed. One prisoner had his front teeth knocked down his throat during interrogation and had to be sent to Prague for an operation.

When Karban was not working at Terezin, he lived with 30 to 35 other people in an unfurnished cell measuring 5 yards by 6 yards. While there Karban witnessed a similar instance to that described by Jech of a Jew being ordered to hang himself by the morning, the S.S. guard on this occasion considerately throwing a rope in the cell for the purpose. On another occasion a Jew was tied onto the back of a lorry by a rope and dragged behind it until he was dead. A former chief inspector of police from Pilsen was tortured by the prison commandant and the Gestapo by having his mouth filled with salt and boiling water poured into it.

NINE WOMEN FROM RAVENSBRUCK

The Czech women who have arrived here have none of them spent less than two and a half years at the Ravensbruck women's concentration camp. One was there for five years. Their ages range from 22 to 53. The oldest, Mrs. Marie Seidlova, was sent to this camp on a charge of having forwarded letters hidden in a parcel to a Czech patriot in the local prison. In some of the larger barracks at Ravensbruck there ~~lived as many as a thousand women,~~ sleeping three or four to a bed. The women of Polish nationality were predominant in the camp, but there was a large number of French women there. The death rate among the French women was high as they were not strong enough to stand the rigours of the life.

HITLER OR GOD?

Prisoners were classified according to their offences, and carried a distinguishing mark on their left sleeve. For political prisoners this was a piece of red cloth, for criminal prisoners green, for Jewesses yellow, prostitutes black, and conscientious objectors on religious grounds purple. These women who wore the purple cloth refused to do any work which might help the war effort of the Reich, and declared that they believed in God and disbelieved in Hitler. They were frequently beaten up in attempts to make them change their views and they were admired by all the other prisoners for their courage.

The only work they would do was domestic work such as cleaning up the guards' barracks. They were free to return home immediately if they were ready to sign a document saying that they believed in Hitler and not in God.

"THE JOURNEY TO HEAVEN"

About twice a month about 300 women at a time were removed from the camp to an adjoining compound on what was known among them as the "journey to heaven". The selections were made by German doctors and always included the older women and every one unfit to work. They were removed and gassed, their bodies being burned in a crematorium, the smoke from which used to pour over the camp with a horrible stench. Some of the younger Czech women, who were employed in carting fuel from the woods to a fuel pile near the gas chamber, on one occasion were able to speak to a male prisoner who was among the few prisoners forced to work in the gas chamber. It was from him that they learned what went on there. 300 people were gassed on Good Friday this year, and as transports were frequently brought from other camps, the crematorium chimneys were smoking all over the Easter holiday for four days.

Gassing was not the only way of despatching prisoners, and the German doctors in the camp hospital frequently killed people with injections while some of the more healthy Polish girls were taken to the hospital and used for surgical experiments. The Germans openly referred to them as "human guinea pigs" and in many cases they were returned to the camp suffering frightful pain and crippled for life.

On Easter Tuesday this year the Germans began to demolish the gas chamber in the hope that the Russians would find no trace when they arrived.

PUNISHMENT

Beatings at this camp were as regular and barbarous as those administered to any male prisoners. The victim was strapped to a wall and beaten by a female warder in the presence of a doctor. If the doctor considered it necessary to stop the beating, the woman was taken to hospital until she was fit enough to receive the balance of her punishment, which was usually anything from 25 to 50 strokes with a rubber truncheon. The penalty for escaping, in addition to a beating, was to have all the hair shorn from the head and in addition the block to which the escapee belonged was often made to stand outside on appel for the whole night.

In addition to deaths caused by the various ingenious forms of German execution, there were also epidemics in the camp causing deaths through dysentry and typhus. The stamina and resistance of the women prisoners was low owing to the food ration, which was far below anything which prisoners of war have known. The daily bread ration which in 1942 was about 370 grams a day, was reduced steadily until about last November it was only 180 grams. A ration of jam amounting to about a soup spoonful was issued twice a week in 1942, later only once a week, and since last November not at all. There was soup or coffee at 3.30 a.m., noon, and in the evening after the day's work which lasted for 13 hours, with one hour break. Just before the Russians reached Ravensbruck, 7,000 women marched west and two or three thousand of them were shot on the road at Wittstock.

A LIMITED NUMBER OF COPIES OF THIS ISSUE IS AVAILABLE IN THE NEWS OFFICE; APPLY BETWEEN 10.00 a.m. AND 12.00 a.m.

1 CANADIAN TRANSIT CAMP (X PW)
Lt-Col Vincent McKenna, MC, ED.
Commanding Officer

- - - - - - - - - - - - - - -

1. WELCOME to #1 Canadian Transit Camp (X PW)

2. OBJECT - to make you as comfortable as possible and to provide an early return to "Blighty".

3. DIAGRAM OF CAMP - see reverse side of this sheet.

4. RECEPTION DRILL - This is laid on in order that you may be immediately ready for despatch as soon as planes are available.

(a) Debus on Square - heavy kit may be left there and picked up later.
(b) Halt for latrines as required.
(c) Medical Inspection.
(d) Documentation.
(e) Pay.
(f) Clothing.
(g) Prepare for showers in the dressing room.
(h) Showers.
(i) Dress in clean clothes and discard old clothing in the receptacles provided.
(j) Red Cross for free issues of cigs, sweets, razor, soap, etc.
(k) Dusting.
(l) Pick up kit left at point "A" and proceed to Coys for quartering - twin beds provided (upper and lower).
(m) Food at last and then freedom to go and come as you please.
(n) Interrogation on a voluntary basis.

5. RECREATIONAL FACILITIES.

(a) Dry Canteen - "Rest Awhile" operated by the British Council of Voluntary Workers and Cdn Auxiliary Services, providing tea, cigs, various games such as ping-pong, etc, writing and reading facilities, plus dance bands or other music.

(b) Wet Canteen - "Half-Way House" operated by this unit. The beer is only a fair substitute for "Mild and Bitter".

(c) Movies or "Flicks", whichever you prefer, are held in the building as noted on the reverse side.

(d) Gift Shops - attractive articles may be purchased at the two "Gift Shops" for your wives, sweethearts or children. One of these is in the dry canteen operated by the Canadian YMCA, and the other, as shown on the diagram, by the Voluntary Army Welfare Services, 21 Army Gp.

6. MONEY EQUIVALENTS

Canadian	English	French	Belgian	Dutch	German
$1.00	£0.4.0.	45 Frs	40 Frs	2 Glds & 37c	9 Marks

7. DEPARTURE

Your stay here will be short - 12 to 48 hours in most cases, and you will then be despatched by air. This unit receives about 1 hour's notice before actual departure, in which time personnel must be notified by loud speaker, collected by serials on the square, issued embarkation cards, (AFSW 3060) in duplicate, embus, given haversack lunch and despatched to the airfield.

There is no desire on the part of this unit to restrict your comings and goings but remember if you are not around when your serial is called, you will miss your plane and must wait over.

BEST OF LUCK, GOD BLESS

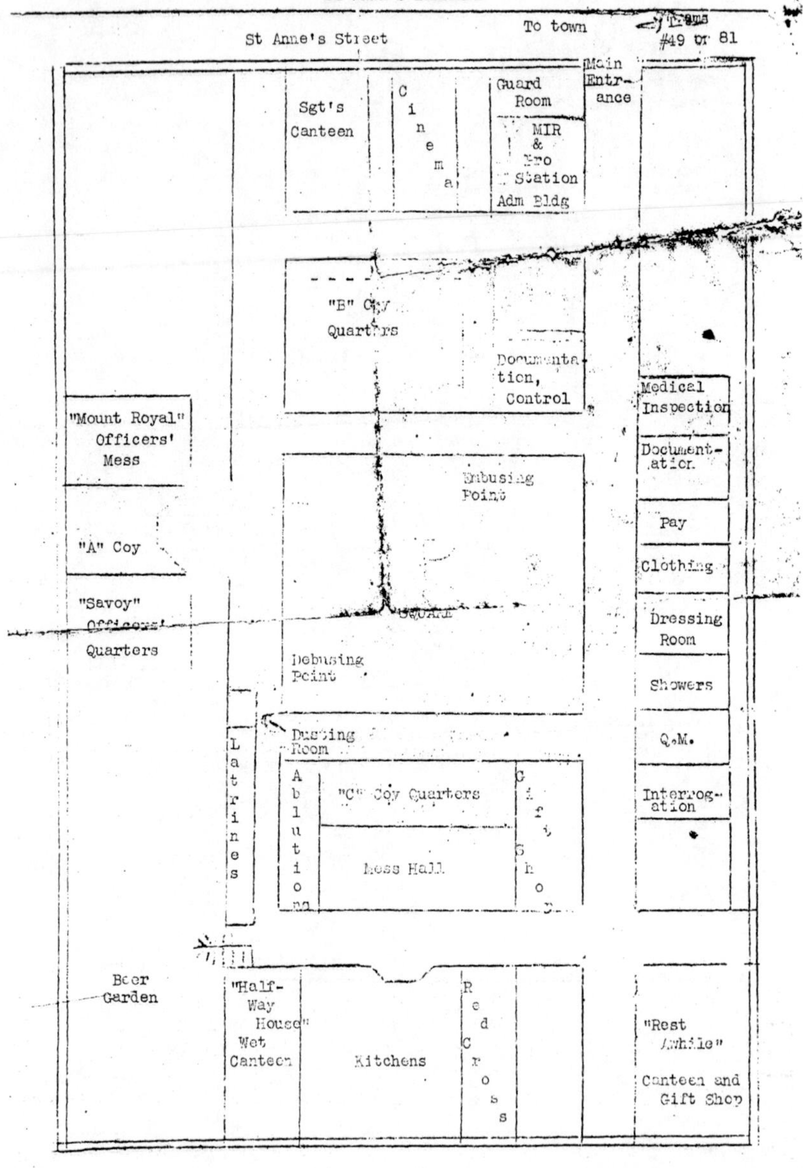
1 CANADIAN TRANSIT CAMP (X IW)
ST ANNE'S BARRACKS
St Anne's Street
To town
Trams #49 or 81
Main Entrance
Sgt's Canteen
Cinema
Guard Room
MIR & Pro Station
Adm Bldg
"B" Coy Quarters
Documentation, Control
Medical Inspection
"Mount Royal" Officers' Mess
Documentation
Embusing Point
Pay
"A" Coy
Clothing
"Savoy" Officers' Quarters
SQUARE
Dressing Room
Debusing Point
Showers
Dusting Room
Q.M.
Latrines
Ablutions
"C" Coy Quarters
Gift Shop
Interrogation
Mess Hall
Beer Garden
"Half-Way House" Wet Canteen
Kitchens
Red Cross
"Rest Awhile" Canteen and Gift Shop

Also published by Woodfield...

The following titles are all available in high-quality softback format

RAF HUMOUR

Bawdy Ballads & Dirty Ditties of the RAF – A huge collection of the bawdy songs and rude recitations beloved by RAF personnel in WW2. Certain to amuse any RAF veteran. Uncensored – so strictly adults only! *"Not for the frail, the fraightfully posh or proper gels – but great fun for everyone else!"* **£9.95**

Upside Down Nothing on the Clock – Dozens of jokes and anecdotes contributed by RAF personnel from AC2s to the top brass... still one of our best sellers. *"Highly enjoyable."* **£6.00**

Upside Down Again! – Our second great collection of RAF jokes, funny stories and anecdotes – a great gift for those with a high-flying sense of humour! *"Very funny indeed."* **£6.00**

Was It Like This For You? – A feast of humorous reminiscences & cartoons depicting the more comical aspects of life in the RAF. *"Will bring back many happy memories. Highly recommended."* **£6.00**

MILITARY MEMOIRS & HISTORIES – THE POST-WAR PERIOD

Flying the Waves **Richard Pike** describes his eventful second career as a commercial helicipter pilot, which involved coastguard Air/Sea Rescue operations in the Shetlands and North Sea. **£9.95**

From Port T to RAF Gan The history of the RAF's most deserted outpost is comprehensively and entertainingly charted by **Peter Doling**, a former RAF officer who served on Gan in the 1970s. Many photos, some in colour. **£14.95**

I Have Control... Former RAF Parachute instructor **Edward Cartner** humorously recalls the many mishaps, blunders and faux-pas of his military career. *Superb writing; very amusing indeed.* **£9.95**

Korea: We Lived They Died Former soldier with Duke of Wellington's Regt **Alan Carter** reveals the appalling truth of front-line life for British troops in this now forgotten war. *Very funny in places too.* **£9.95**

Meteor Eject! Former 257 Sqn pilot [1950s] **Nick Carter** recalls the early days of RAF jets and his many adventures flying Meteors, including one very lucky escape via a Mk.2 Martin-Baker ejector seat... **£9.95**

Pluck Under Fire Eventful Korean War experiences of **John Pluck** with the Middlesex Regiment **£9.95**

Return to Gan Michael Butler's light-hearted account of life at RAF Gan in 1960 and the founding of 'Radio Gan'. *Will delight those who also served at this remote RAF outpost in the Indian Ocean.* **£12.00**

The Spice of Flight Former RAF pilot **Richard Pike** delivers a fascinating account of flying Lightnings, Phantoms and later helicopters with 56, 43(F) & 19 Sqns in the RAF of the 1960s & 70s. **£9.95**

Tread Lightly into Danger Bomb-disposal expert **Anthony Charlwood**'s experiences in some of the world's most dangerous hotspots (Kuwait, Iraq, Lebanon, Somalia, etc) over the last 30 years. **£9.95**

Who is in Charge Here...? Former RAF Parachute instructor **Edward Cartner** regales us with more inglorious moments from the latter part of his military career as a senior officer. *Superb writing; very amusing indeed.* **£9.95**

MILITARY MEMOIRS & HISTORIES – WORLD WAR 1 & 2

2297: A POW's Story Taken prisoner at Dunkirk, **John Lawrence** spent 5 years as a POW at Lamsdorf, Jagendorf, Posen and elsewhere. *"A very interesting & delightfully illustrated account of his experiences."* **£6.00**

A Bird Over Berlin Former Lancaster pilot with 61 Sqn, **Tony Bird DFC** tells a remarkable tale of survival against the odds during raids on the German capital & as a POW. *"An incredible-but-true sequence of events."* **£9.95**

A Journey from Blandford The wartime exploits of motorcycle dispatch rider **B.A. Jones** began at Blandford Camp in Dorset but took him to Dunkirk, the Middle East, D-Day and beyond... **£9.95**

A Lighter Shade of Blue A former Radar Operator **Reg O'Neil** recalls his WW2 service in Malta and Italy with 16004 AMES – a front-line mobile radar unit. *'Interesting, informative and amusing.'* **£9.95**

A Shilling's Worth of Promises Delightfully funny memoirs of **Fred Hitchcock,** recalling his years as an RAF airman during the war and later amusing escapades in the UK and Egypt. *A very entertaining read.* **£9.95**

Beaufighters BOAC & Me – WW2 Beaufighter navigator **Sam Wright** served a full tour with 254 Sqn and was later seconded to BOAC on early postwar overseas routes. *'Captures the spirit of the Beaufighter'* **£9.95**

Coastal Command Pilot Former Hudson pilot **Ted Rayner**'s outstanding account of his unusual WW2 Coastal Command experiences, flying in the Arctic from bases in Iceland and Greenland. **£9.95**

Cyril Wild: The Tall Man Who Never Slept – **James Bradley**'s biography of a remarkable Japanese-speaking British Army officer who helped many POWs survive on the infamous Burma railway. **£9.95**

***Desert War Diary* by John Walton** Diary and photos recording the activities of the Hurricanes and personnel of 213 Squadron during WW2 in Cyprus and Egypt. *"Informative and entertaining."* **£9.95**

From Fiji to Balkan Skies Spitfire/Mustang pilot **Dennis McCaig** recalls eventful WW2 operations over the Adriatic/Balkans with 249 Sqn in 43/44. *'A rip-roaring real-life adventure, splendidly written.'* **£9.95**

From Horses to Chieftains – Long-serving Army veteran **Richard Napier** recalls an eventful Army career that began with a cavalry regiment in 1935; took in El Alamein & D-Day and ended in the 1960s. **£9.95**

Get Some In! The many wartime adventures of **Mervyn Base**, a WW2 RAF Bomb Disposal expert **£9.95**

Just a Survivor Former Lancaster navigator **Phil Potts** tells his remarkable tale of survival against the odds in the air with 103 Sqn and later as a POW. *'An enlightening and well written account.'* **£9.95**

Memoirs of a 'Goldfish' • The eventful wartime memoirs of former 115 Sqn Wellington pilot **Jim Burtt-Smith**, now president of the Goldfish Club - exclusively for aviators who have force-landed into water. **£9.95**

Nobody Unprepared – The history of No 78 Sqn RAF is told in full for the first time by **Vernon Holland** in this absorbing account of the Whitley/Halifax squadron's World War 2 exploits. Full statistics and roll of honour. **£14.95**

No Brylcreem, No Medals – RAF MT driver **Jack Hambleton** 's splendid account of his wartime escapades in England, Shetlands & Middle East blends comic/tragic aspects of war in uniquely entertaining way. **£9.95**

Nobody's Hero • Former RAF Policeman **Bernard Hart-Hallam**'s extraordinary adventures with 2TAF Security Section on D-Day and beyond in France, Belgium & Germany. *"Unique and frequently surprising."* **£9.95**

Once a Cameron Highlander • This biog of Robert Burns, who, at 104 was the oldest survivor of the Battle of the Somme; takes in his WW1 experiences, later life in showbusiness and celebrity status as a centenarian. **£9.95**

Operation Pharos • **Ken Rosam** tells the story of the RAF's secret bomber base/staging post on the Cocos Keeling islands during WW2 and of many operations from there. *'A fascinating slice of RAF history.'* **£9.95**

Over Hell & High Water • WW2 navigator **Les Parsons** survived 31 ops on Lancasters with 622 Sqn, then went on to fly Liberators in Far East with 99 Sqn. *'An exceptional tale of 'double jeopardy'.* **£9.95**

Pacifist to Glider Pilot • The son of Plymouth Brethren parents, **Alec Waldron** renounced their pacifism and went on to pilot gliders with the Glider Pilot Regiment at both Sicily & Arnhem. *Excellent photos.* **£9.95**

Pathfinder Force Balkans • Pathfinder F/Engineer **Geoff Curtis** saw action over Germany & Italy before baling out over Hungary. He was a POW in Komarno, Stalags 17a & 17b. *'An amazing catalogue of adventures.'* **£9.95**

Per Ardua Pro Patria • Humour and tragedy are interwoven in these unassuming autobiographical observations of **Dennis Wiltshire**, a former Lancaster Flight Engineer who later worked for NASA. **£9.95**

Ploughs, Planes & Palliasses • Entertaining recollections of RAF pilot **Percy Carruthers**, who flew Baltimores in Egypt with 223 Squadron and was later a POW at Stalag Luft 1 & 6. **£9.95**

RAF/UXB The Story of RAF Bomb Disposal • Stories contributed by wartime RAF BD veterans that will surprise and educate the uninitiated. *"Amazing stories of very brave men."* **£9.95**

Railway to Runway • Wartime diary & letters of Halifax Observer **Leslie Harris** – killed in action with 76 Sqn in 1943 – poignantly capture the spirit of the wartime RAF in the words of a 20-year-old airman. **£9.95**

Seletar Crowning Glory • The history of the RAF base in Singapore from its earliest beginnings, through the golden era of the flying-boats, its capture in WW2 and on to its closure in the 1970s. **£15.00**

The RAF & Me • Former Stirling navigator **Gordon Frost** recalls ops with 570 Sqn from RAF Harwell, including 'Market-Garden' 'Varsity' and others. *'A salute to the mighty Stirling and its valiant crews.'* **£9.95**

Training for Triumph • **Tom Docherty**'s very thorough account of the amazing achievement of RAF Training Command, who trained over 90,000 aircrew during World War 2. *'An impressively detailed book.'* **£12.00**

To Strive and Not to Yield An inspiring account of the involvement of No 626 Squadron RAF Bomber Command in the 'Battle of Berlin' (1943/44) and a salute to the men and women who served on the squadron. **£14.95**

Un Grand Bordel • Geoffrey French relates air-gunner **Norman Lee**'s amazing real-life adventures with the French Maquis (Secret Army) after being shot down over Europe. *"Frequently funny and highly eventful."* **£9.95**

UXB Vol 2 More unusual and gripping tales of bomb disposal in WW2 and after. **£9.95**

Wot! No Engines? • Alan Cooper tells the story of military gliders in general and the RAF glider pilots who served on Operation Varsity in 1945 in particular. A very large and impressive book with many photos. **£18.00**

While Others Slept • Former Hampden navigator **Eric Woods** tells the story of Bomber Command's early years and how he completed a tour of duty with 144 Squadron. *'Full of valuable historical detail.'* **£9.95**

WOMEN & WORLD WAR TWO

A WAAF at War • Former MT driver **Diana Lindo**'s charming evocation of life in the WAAF will bring back happy memories to all those who also served in World War 2. *"Nostalgic and good-natured."* **£9.95**

Corduroy Days • Warm-hearted and amusing recollections of **Josephine Duggan-Rees**'s wartime years spent as a Land Girl on farms in the New Forest area. *"Funny, nostalgic and very well written."* **£9.95**

Ernie • **Celia Savage**'s quest to discover the truth about the death of her father, an RAF Halifax navigator with 149 Sqn, who died in WW2 when she was just 6 years old. *"A real-life detective story."* **£9.95**

In My Father's Footsteps • **Pat Bienkowski**'s moving account of her trip to Singapore & Thailand to visit the places where her father and uncle were both POW's during WW2. **£9.95**

Lambs in Blue • **Rebecca Barnett's** revealing account of the wartime lives and loves of a group of WAAFs posted to the tropical paradise of Ceylon. *"A highly congenial WW2 chronicle."* **£9.95**

Radar Days • Delightful evocation of life in the wartime WAAF by former Radar Operator **Gwen Arnold**, who served at Bawdsey Manor RDF Station, Suffolk. *"Amusing, charming and affectionate."* **£9.95**

Searching in the Dark The amusing wartime diary of **Peggy Butler** a WAAF radar operator 1942-1946 – written when she was just 19 yrs old and serving at Bawdsey RDF station in Suffolk **£9.95**

MEMOIRS & HISTORIES – NON-MILITARY

20th CenturyFarmers Boy • Sussex farmer **Nick Adames** looks back on a century of rural change and what it has meant to his own family and the county they have farmed in for 400 years. **£9.95**

Call an Ambulance! • former ambulance driver **Alan Crosskill** recalls a number of light-hearted episodes from his eventful career in the 1960s/70s. *'Very amusing and entertaining'.* **£9.95**

Harry – An Evacuee's Story • The misadventures of **Harry Collins** – a young lad evacuated from his home in Stockport UK to Manitoba, Canada in WW2. *'An educational description of the life of an evacuee'* **£9.95**

Just Visiting... • Charming and funny book by former Health Visitor **Molly Corbally**, who brilliantly depicts colourful characters and entertaining incidents from her long career. **£9.95**

Occupation Nurse • **Peter & Mary Birchenall** pay tribute to the achievement of the group of untrained nurses who provided healthcare at Guernsey's only hospital during the German occupation of 1940-45. **£9.95**

FICTION

A Trace of Calcium by **David Barnett** – A commuter comes to the aid of a young woman in trouble, becomes implicated in murder and must use all his resources to clear his name. **£9.95**

Double Time **by David Barnett** – A light-hearted time-travel fantasy in which a bookmaker tries to use a time machine to make his fortune and improve his love-life with hilarious consequences. **£9.95**

Last Sunset by **AA Painter** A nautical thriller set in the world of international yachting. A middle aged yachtsman becomes accidentally embroiled with smugglers, pirates and a very sexy young lady... **£9.95**

The Brats by **Tony Paul** Tony Paul tells the true story of his grandfather, who, as a boy, along with several friends, stowed away on a ship bound for Canada. The youngsters' brutal mistreatment at the hands of the Captain and Mate of the ship caused a scandal that made headlines in Victorian times. *An enthralling real-life seafaring story.* **£9.95**

The Cherkassy Incident by **Hunter Carlyle** A gripping action thriller featuring a terrorist plot to steal nuclear missiles from a sunken Russian nuclear submarine and the efforts of international security agents to stop them. **£9.95**

MISCELLANEOUS SUBJECTS

Just a Butcher's Boy by **Christopher Bolton** Charming account of small town life in the 1950s in the rural Leiston, Suffolk and idyllic summers spent with grandparents who owned the local butcher's shop. **£5.95**

Impress of Eternity by **Paul McNamee** An investigation into the authenticity of the Turin Shroud. A former schoolmaster examines the evidence and comes to a startling conclusion. **£5.95**

Making a Successful Best Man's Speech An indispensable aid to anyone who feels nervous about making a wedding speech. Tells you what to say and how to remember it. **£5.95**

Near & Yet So Far by **Audrey Truswell** The founder of an animal rescue charity tells charming and heart-warming tales of the rescue and rehabilitation of many four-legged friends in need. **£9.95**

Reputedly Haunted Inns of the Chilterns & Thames Valley by **Roger Long** – A light hearted look at pubs & the paranormal in the Heart of England **£5.95**

BOOKS FEATURING THE SOUTH COAST & THE SOUTH DOWNS REGION

A Portrait of Slindon by **Josephine Duggan Rees** A charming history of this attractive and well-preserved West Sussex village, from its earliest beginnings to the present day, taking in the exploits of its many notable residents over the years. Very informative and entertaining. Illustrated with many photos, some in colour. **£14.95**

Retribution by **Mike Jupp** An outrageous and very funny comedy/fantasy novel for adults and older children, featuring bizarre goings-on in a quiet English seaside town that bears a striking resemblance to Mike's home town of Bognor Regis. Brilliantly illustrated. **£9.95**

Unknown to History and Fame by **Brenda Dixon** – Charming portrait of Victorian life in the West Sussex village of Walberton via the writings of Charles Ayling, a resident of the village, whose reports on local events were a popular feature in *The West Sussex Gazette* over many years during the Victorian era. **£9.95**

A Little School on the Downs The story of Harriet Finlay-Johnson, headmistress of a little school junior in Sompting, West Sussex in the 1890s, whose ideas and classroom techniques began a revolution in education. She also scandalised society at the time by marrying a former pupil, 20 years her junior. *An amazing and inspiring true story.* **£9.95**

The South Coast Beat Scene of the 1960s The South Coast may not have been as famous as Liverpool in the swinging sixties but it was nevertheless a hotbed of musical activity. Broadcaster **Mike Read** traces the complete history of the musicians, the fans and the venues from Brighton to Bognor in this large and lavishly illustrated book. **£24.95**

Boys & Other Animals by **Josephine Duggan Rees**. A charming and delightfully funny account of a mother's many trials and tribulations bringing up a boisterous all-male family on a farm in rural Sussex during the 1950s-70s. **£9.95**

Woodfield books are available direct from the publishers by mail order

Telephone your orders to (**+44** if outside UK) **01243** 821234

Fax orders your to (**+44** if outside UK) **01243** 821757

All major credit cards accepted.

Visit our website for full details of all our titles where instant online ordering is available:

www.woodfieldpublishing.com

Full money-back guarantee: If you are not satisfied with any of our books, simply return them to us in good condition and we will refund your money, no questions asked.